Praise for Bob Cancalosi

"Courageous leaders are authentic. They lead aligned with their values, inspire trust, and are adept at creating a climate where others can shine, take risks, and do their absolute best work. Courageous leaders lean into adversity and hold individuals accountable, all the while removing barriers to others' success. Courageous leaders foster a strong sense of team, recognize and reward performance, and when needed, make the tough calls.

"I've known Bob Cancalosi for 16 years and have had the pleasure at GE Crotonville of working both for and with him. Through the years, Bob has been my champion, encouraged me to take risks and swing big while always striving toward the betterment of myself and the team. Bob epitomizes the courageous leader, and I am all the better for having served under his leadership and worked by his side. I now have the honor to call him a dear and lifelong friend."

~ **RICH BRAATEN**
—Regional Learning Leader—The Americas—GE Crotonville

"I define courage as having the mental strength to venture and persevere in the face of fear, difficulty, or uncertainty. One way leaders can increase their mental strength is by learning to balance action and reflection. Over the almost three decades I worked with Bob, one constant I observed was a willingness to try, to be in action, even when unsure how to act or what might happen. To be sure, not everything was a success. As he once said to me, 'I've taken a lot of hits.' At the same time, Bob has been purposeful, some might say maniacal, in thinking about and writing down what happened, what he learned, and what might be a new approach.

Bob is a longtime practitioner in the art of balancing action and reflection, and his book is a thoughtful and useful guide for leaders looking to improve their mental strength."

~ **NICK CAFFENTZIS**
—Former GE Healthcare Digital CMO & Senior Fellow & Executive Director, Kellogg Chief Marketing Officer Program, Northwestern University

"I love the definition of courage. The ability to do something that frightens someone. Many assume leaders do big bold things because they aren't afraid. In my personal experience, this couldn't be further from the truth when it comes to leadership. Real leadership is using tools to help us do the thing we are passionate about, even if we are scared out of our minds. But we need the tools and training to help us. Bob's book and his example have been a guiding force to help so many be courageous. The lessons he teaches us will be life changing when it comes to leading courageously."

~ **KRISTI HAYES**
—Founder, Be Strong Story, Author, Podcast Host

"I met Bob Cancalosi at a global leadership program in 2017. His was the only talk in seven weeks that resulted in a standing ovation. More significantly, there was not a dry eye left in the room when he finished talking. On reflection, the reason Bob impacted the audience so deeply is that it clearly took courage for him to talk to us from the heart.

"Bob often reminds leaders that to be successful and impactful, they must show what is in their own hearts and connect with the hearts of the people around them. As a leader, it takes real courage to admit that you do not have the answer or are feeling unsure. Bob believes and declares that leaders should be honest and authentic as a way of helping to build trust with the people depending on them. That foundation of honesty, authenticity, and trust can help organizations achieve any goal and pass any test that awaits.

"In these historically unsettled times, individuals have ever-increasing expectations for their leaders to provide clarity and direction. In the face of significant uncertainty, leaders still are expected to steer their organizations. Leaders will need new reserves of courage to navigate challenges previously unseen, if not unimagined. Luckily, leaders have at their disposal the head, hands, and heart of Bob Cancalosi and his daughter, Alessandra. With Bob and Alessandra's powerful perspectives to guide them, leaders with the courage to lead are well-positioned to succeed."

~ **JOHN KREUP**
—Energy Industry Executive and HBS AMP Graduate

"What can I say about Bob? He is intelligent, wise, witty, articulate, a source of answers, a family man, and just an all-around great person and friend. He has skilled all these attributes to become a successful business-

man, author, and entrepreneur. As a family man, I also appreciate his courage that he bestows upon his children, and his youngest daughter, Alessandra, as co-author is proof. I have nothing but admiration and respect for anyone who can put pen to paper and succeed. I commend you, Bob, for having the discipline and energy necessary to frame and finish your writing project, despite all the other demands on you. Knowing Bob has made me a better person, friend, listener, and husband. Thank you, Bob, you have shown me what great courage is in the face of turbulence and pain."

~ **TIM KUBINA**
—Marketing Executive

"To successfully lead in all aspects of your professional or personal life, you must commit to constant and consistent displays of courage. Courageous people believe in themselves; they are passionate, purposeful, and willing to drive change. I have been blessed to know, learn, and evolve by witnessing Bob's overt and covert displays of courage for more than 20 years. Bob never fails to approach life with action, passion, and perseverance. Bob acts, and he inspires others to do the same. Bob has inspired and instilled his courage and passion onto his friends and family—most notably, his daughter and co-author, Alessandra, who through her education and work will ensure our world remains sustainable and becomes a better place. We all need reminders of how to act courageously, be passionate, and act; this book will help us to all be better in the face of change or turmoil."

~ **KATHY MCCORMACK**
—Communications Executive

"Our world is begging for courageous leadership in business, government and society. Without courage, leadership lies dormant amidst so many who have compelling reasons to lead! Leadership and learning expert Bob Cancalosi, and daughter Alessandra Cancalosi, a trailblazer in sustainable agriculture, present a robust way for each of us to grow our courage to lead. Their model, developed under the scrutiny of experience, reflection, education, and generational perspective and debate, is there for anyone who agrees there could be no better time to raise the standard on leadership."

~ **TONI M. PRISTO, PH.D.**
—Principal, Pristo Consulting

"It takes courage to have courage, let alone lead yourself, let alone lead others. The very word courage means 'of the heart; the seat of feelings,' just as a cri de cœur means a cry from the heart. To me, courage is the guts, the grit, to carry a dream, a hope, a wish forward, in such a way that others willfully follow. In Courage to Lead, Bob Cancalosi leads you over the bed of hot coals that spells out courage. Seven letters that can terrify if taken singly rather than together. Like marathons, courage always seems to be something enviable once you are safely past it—but while you are in the throes of testing it, few miseries can compare. Bob is like a Sherpa guide, ready to get you through the low-oxygen, altitude sickness climbs (and descents) around progress—your personal Mount Everest. As Bob's longtime childhood neighbor and friend, I witnessed this firsthand. Where the words end, the examples begin, and when you demonstrate the courage to lead, the examples themselves never end. Instead, they forge an ironclad legacy; a living bridge between past and future. I hope you will enjoy the view from that bridge as much as I have."

~ANDY O'HEARN
—Associate Director, Communications and Change Management

"One of the gifts of Bob Cancalosi is that he seems to be fearless in the face of discovery; in fact, he relishes the taste of it. He invites us to face our fears so that we might be discoverers of new ways of learning, while at the same time finding new ways of living. I invite you to enjoy these new ways that are clearly Bob's and now clearly ours, because he is so generous to offer them to us.

"Bob has a particularly important gift of keeping things simple or bringing things that might be very complex into simple ways of seeing them, of developing metaphor and means, of making our way into understanding together. A good teacher, I believe, not only points the way to what is but leads us into the questions that will take us to what might be.

"You may have grown up self-reflective, or you may have grown up in systems where persons were occasionally frightened by the possibility of self-reflection. The inner world of becoming is where we discover truths that will both challenge and lead our lives and nourish us to serve the world around us.

"With no artificial sheen or shine, Bob glows in such a way as to bring others into the goodness and giftedness he sees and believes in. His generous heart wants you and me to know some things that will both benefit us and help our world to be a better place for everyone. Both from systems to ourselves, from hierarchies to circles of gathering, Bob has insights.

"Listen, be curious, open your heart, and let the richness of his book and the urgency of the world around us give us energy for transformation. Bob continues to offer stories, practices, and insights that give us hope. With his Franciscan heart, he might follow in the footsteps of St. Francis of Assisi, who said. 'Up until now we have done very little, let us begin again!'"

~ DANIEL RILEY
—OFM, Founder/Animator, Mt. Irenaeus

"We need leaders who can make the tough decisions, hold people accountable, and maintain resilience through it all. Bob's insights and clear models are a memorable guide for leaders at all levels looking to increase their courageous leadership capabilities."

~ AMY SPERANZA
—Director of GE Advanced Leadership Development Programs

"Courage is one of those invisible topics that is only brought to life through living courageously.

My experience, so far, of living courageously is this: every step is uncertain, impactful, and requires a balanced head, heart, and guts. Even so, every step is also full of possibilities, taken with a conscious support team in place to both celebrate the high and support the low.

"My experience of Bob Cancalosi is that he is a PRO at living courageously. He has more 'reps' at courage than most. What takes Bob from the Hall of Fame to being a legend at the game of courage is that he learned for himself and then has relentlessly committed his life to serving others. I am a grateful student of Bob's courage—his writing and teaching is straight from the school of experience and perseverance."

~ SANDY SULLIVAN
—20-YEAR COLLEAGUE OF BOB CANCALOSI
Founder and Partner of The Alchemy Group

"As a leader, I don't always feel courageous. Like many, I can fall prey to the uncertainties of these days. But leadership doesn't allow time to sit back in fear of the unknown. I move forward, blazing a trail for others to follow. 'Courage is resistance to fear, mastery of fear—not absence of fear.' [Mark Twain] With other people depending on me to lead them, I dig deep within for courage. And at the end of my capabilities, I draw courage from a source beyond me. My strength to persevere isn't from courage, but from passion and faith."

~ LISA M. UMINA
—Publisher and Award-winning Author

"Courage in leadership is showing no fear. It is a characteristic worthy of the utmost admiration. When a leader exhibits courage, he or she gains instant respect and loyalty from those he or she guides. With this combination of powerful ingredients, success for the entire team is certain to follow.

"The many business owners, entrepreneurs, and corporate executives I have met throughout my career all seem to have what I like to refer to as 'the Teflon effect.' Nothing ever seems to stick to them. They have the ability to easily brush off fear, uncertainty, and negativity and simply forge ahead without looking back to accomplish greatness. William Faulkner once said, 'You cannot swim for new horizons until you have the courage to lose sight of the shore.' This is the Teflon effect I am referring to.

"I have known Bob now for more than 20 years. During this time, I have been fortunate to witness his courageous leadership, 'Teflon effect,' and fortitude in both the corporate setting and in his family life. He has always shown the courage to move forward without fear and never lets any obstacles stand in his way. In fact, when he faces a new obstacle, he looks upon it as a challenge and an opportunity to share his experiences with others.

"When we first met, Bob and I had recently been recruited to co-lead our sons' Cub Scout Pack. I quickly realized how incredibly lucky these young boys were to have Bob as one of their leaders. With Bob's busy schedule during that time, it would have been very easy for him to decline this time-consuming volunteer role. Most people in that situation would have simply passed the buck and let another parent step up to the task.

"The courage Bob showed in taking on that role so many years ago, and now in his new role as author and consultant, has certainly made me contemplate my own courage and challenges over the past few decades. Without a doubt, my friendship with Bob has made me a better person, and I thank him for his wisdom and camaraderie—as well as for allowing me to witness his faith and perseverance through unimaginable personal challenges. As you read Bob's latest book, I hope you can appreciate his *insight and learn from his experiences to find the courage to share your talents, wisdom, and journey with those that matter in your life."*

~ JOHN WITTAK
—Retired Marketing/Media Executive

"We are living in times that are asking us, perhaps demanding us, to show up courageously. And courage is not always easy. In fact, it rarely is. To be courageous means you lean into discomfort with an open heart and an open mind. It is less about sharing what you know, and more about being open to what you do not know. Intention matters, but outcomes matter more, and accountability matters most. Courage is not limited to leaders but rather is what good leaders are in large part made of. Thank you, Bob, for writing a book about this important topic and for showing us the way."

~ JACQUELIN ZEHNER
—Co-Founder, Women Moving Millions, and Former Partner and Managing Director at Goldman Sachs

"Many books are available on moving ahead in life despite feelings of despair or fear. Bob's latest book, Courage to Lead, is not just a book to read and absorb; it's a practical, user-friendly tool for all of us to use as a 'guidepost' in life. A guide to becoming more open to learning, to progressing as a leader in business, and as a member of our communities—and important today, to find the courage to move forward in mindful and positive ways.

"Adversity in life throws all of us a curveball now and then—it is our choice how we use these experiences to find our courage—our ability to lead and move forward. The practice of journaling to chronicle these experiences is something I'd known about for a long time but never thought would be beneficial or valuable. I was so wrong. Bob's clear instructions, guidance, and personal examples enabled me to start journaling immediately and quite easily. I found early on in the use of this valuable tool that whether it was a mere two minutes or an hour to reflect in my daily journal, day by day it became easier and easier, and I became increasingly more honest with myself.

"My thoughts and reflections on all of it—fears, vulnerabilities, and accomplishments—allowed me to change my own mindset. Those subtle changes in my thinking actually did something I never imagined could be

so powerful each day: a shift in my thought process. Journaling led me to approach each aspect of my life with more thought, insight, and power. My own thoughts, and ability to then reflect on those thoughts, enabled me to become a better leader, a healthier and more loving partner, and a more courageous human being.

"By learning from Bob, one of the best leaders and teachers I know, I promise you will find your own courage, enabling you to be a better leader in all aspects of life!"

~ **LORI ZETLIN-ROSMARIN**
—CEO, Speaker Services

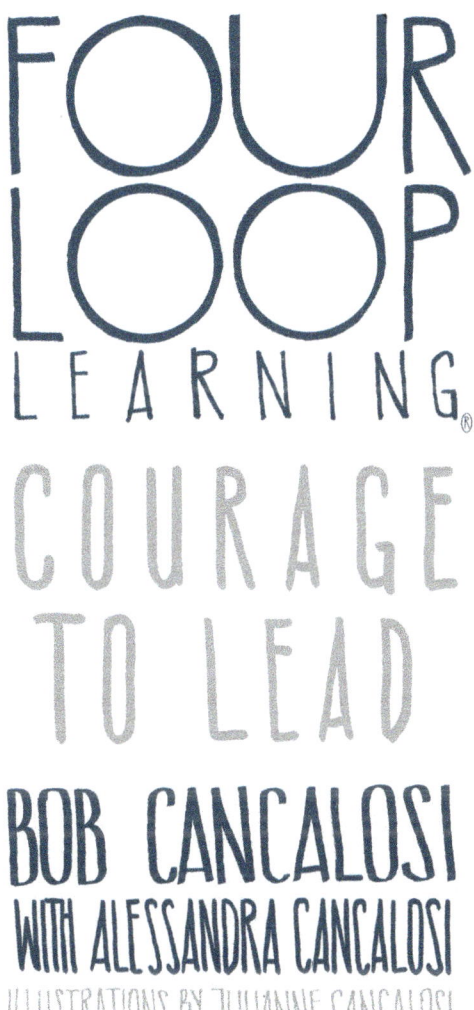

FOUR LOOP LEARNING®

COURAGE TO LEAD

BOB CANCALOSI
WITH ALESSANDRA CANCALOSI
ILLUSTRATIONS BY JULIANNE CANCALOSI

Four Loop Learning: Courage to Lead
Copyright © 2021 Bob Cancalosi with Alessandra Cancalosi
All rights reserved.

No part of this book may be reproduced in any manner whatsoever without the prior written permission of the publisher, except in the case of brief quotations embodied in reviews.

ISBN: 978-1-61244-937-1
LCCN: 2020921242

Halo Publishing International, LLC
8000 W Interstate 10, Suite 600
San Antonio, Texas 78230
www.halopublishing.com

Printed and bound in the United States of America

Dedication

This book is dedicated to the heroes in our world who are demonstrating COURAGE daily to help with some of the biggest challenges we all face today. These are the frontline professionals, doctors and nurses who are delivering exceptional care during the pandemic. They are also the courageous people who are peacefully marching for justice and equality. And finally, for my family and courageous wife, Barbara, who is always by my side and helps me daily as I continue to battle the side effects of a rare head and neck cancer.

CONTENTS

FOREWORD—BY JOHN WISDOM	17
AUTHORS OVERVIEW	21
ALESSANDRA MARIE CANCALOSI	23

CHAPTER ONE:
THE ORIGINS OF COURAGE TO LEAD — 26

CHAPTER TWO:
THE FIVE FUNDAMENTAL CHALLENGES — 34

CHAPTER THREE:
THE SEVEN COMPONENTS OF COURAGE — 48

CHAPTER FOUR:
CHANGE MANAGEMENT AS A CORE COMPETENCY — 52

CHAPTER FIVE:
OVERCOME MENTAL CHATTER — 62

CHAPTER SIX:
USE INFLUENCE — 74

CHAPTER SEVEN:
RELENTLESSLY CONNECT TO PEOPLE'S HEARTS — 82

CHAPTER EIGHT:
ALWAYS LOOK TO IMPROVE — 92

CHAPTER NINE:
    GET REALLY GOOD AT IMPLEMENTATION   104

CHAPTER TEN:
    ENCOURAGE ITERATION, NOT PERFECTION   112

CHAPTER ELEVEN:
    EXAMPLE OF COURAGE IN HEALTHCARE   126

CHAPTER TWELVE:
    THE POWER OF REFLECTION   132

CHAPTER THIRTEEN:
    COMMONLY ASKED QUESTIONS   136

CHAPTER FOURTEEN:
    CONCLUSION   152

NOTES   157

ACKNOWLEDGEMENTS   167

FOREWORD
JOHN WISDOM

How often do you think about courage? We certainly admire it when we see it. Yet we typically associate courage with moments, acts of bravery on stages of all sizes: giving a talk, facing a medical diagnosis, welcoming a new class of students, helping a business find a more purposeful path. From a leadership standpoint, however, courage can be a constant and a tremendous catalyst for learning and growth. This everyday courage is not merely summoned—it's shared. And it enables a leader to have far greater impact in any situation, especially in situations that might otherwise appear routine.

Bob Cancalosi and I first spoke because he was reaching out to help me. *(Those who know him will not be surprised at all by this.)* Bob had just joined the senior staff at Crotonville, GE's leadership institute, after serving as Chief Learning Officer for GE Healthcare for seven years, and was setting out to expand the global customer education program for GE. Which is to say, he already had plenty to do. Yet there he was, bringing ideas, energy, curiosity—generously channeling his play-to-the-rafters, audience-moving vitality into a quiet bit of coaching and tremendous confidence that *we* would solve my issue.

Four Loop Learning: Courage to Lead

There is a world of difference between the leader who wants things *from* you and the leader who wants things *for* you. Bob is clearly in that latter and all-too-rare group. He and I would go on to have many conversations on the Crotonville campus—at customer summits, in team meetings, or just catching up over coffee. And what I observed when we first met held true and remains true to this day. Bob always shows up ready and able to make everyone else better.

During a tough time in my life, Bob was of course one of the people I wanted to talk to right away. Many of us are fortunate to have friends like that: they listen, they offer sympathy and encouragement, they help us move forward. My call with Bob covered that territory as well, in the beginning. But then Bob said something I'll never forget. "Brother, I hope you have a pen and paper handy, because I'd like to share the 10 things you should consider doing next." It was an astonishing statement of support, of optimism, of *courage,* and a reminder that even in the most challenging times, we have choices, actions to take, lessons to learn, possibilities to consider.

We, all of us, are in such a time right now. Governmental institutions are faltering, unable to meet the rightful expectations of a just society or the stewardship requirements of our precious planet. Businesses, organizations, and individuals have an opportunity, and an obligation, to do more. To contribute, to effect meaningful change, however, we will need to think and act differently, finding new levels of courage in the way we organize ourselves and share ideas. And this is where Alessandra Cancalosi offers such an essential voice and vision along with Bob's. Alessandra points us to a future worth earning. How best to pull together and move forward? Progress demands that we now take it upon ourselves to create the roadmap—sustainably, equitably, and humanely.

Courage, in the end, is not about being fearless. It's about being selfless. It allows us to look within, deeply and honestly, as

Foreword

we reflect on what we wish to achieve. Even more importantly, it liberates us to look beyond, to see the potential in others, and to reach out free of ego.

Imagine what you could do with just a bit more courage. Better yet, imagine if courage became an abundant, empowering, transformative constant in your life. What would you create? What risks would you take? What obstacles might you overcome? How many loved ones, colleagues, and communities would you lift up?

You're about to find out.

John

John Wisdom
Senior Vice President,
Global Corporate Practice
Weber Shandwick

AUTHORS OVERVIEW

BOB CANCALOSI AND THE STANDARD PRACTICE OF JOURNALING

I've been journaling an average of 2.7 hours (162 minutes) a day for the past 20 years. As I write this book, I am on Journal #80 and still very much enjoy the mental stimulation of writing, creating, and reflecting. My defining moment to begin journaling started after reading the book *Outliers: The Story of Success* by Malcolm Gladwell (2008) where his research revealed that it takes 10,000 hours or 10 years to become an expert in your field. I was always interested in the theories and practices of leadership development and wanted to gain some expertise. I thought that writing daily in journals was a way to start building some deep domain expertise and strong mental muscle. I would have never predicted I'd be doing it for more than 20 years. Now, with no foreseeable plan to stop, it is a deeply embedded standard practice in how I learn and teach others. The witness of my children using journals, and their use of deliberate reflection to help them unlock even more of their own personal potential, was an unintended bonus.

ALESSANDRA MARIE CANCALOSI

Alessandra is the youngest Cancalosi child, the parents' close favorite behind Surrey, the 13-year-old standard poodle. Alessandra is a current master's degree student at Tufts University's Friedman School of Nutrition Science & Policy, in the Agriculture, Food and Environment Program. She is passionate about sustainable food systems and has spent  the past few years diving into the heart of conservation, pollinator and edible insect research as well as regional supply chain work across the Midwest and New England. Alessandra's perspective on her goals and accomplishments has been deeply ingrained by Bob's leadership practices and learnings throughout her childhood. The opportunity to write a book to share with others alongside her Dad–to bring a millennial perspective and the insights she's found through long conversations at the fireplace with her Dad–is an honor–*as well as* a wonderful reason to enjoy fine wine together.

Alessandra and Bob co-writing the book in Oconomowoc, WI.

THE ORIGINS OF COURAGE TO LEAD

My life has been shaped by incredible forces, bringing the word 'courage' to a deeper meaning than I had ever considered. Given a recent, personal, unexpected journey of adversity—a global pandemic and a reconciling and impeccable social justice movement—it is clear that the world is in need of courageous leaders.

My experiences, and the opportunity to emphasize the profound and powerful leadership we are seeing today, allows me to show how courage can help leaders address unprecedented challenges, which are sometimes complicated by systemic racism. Any leader, and every leader, has an individual duty to use a platform and to continuously self-develop and self-educate on what courageous leadership looks like every day.

PERSONAL EXAMPLE OF COURAGE

Over the past three years, I have struggled with a very rare head and neck cancer: one that required eight major surgeries, proton beam radiation, and chemotherapy. I can happily say that, through these major challenges, I am cancer-free as I write this. The art of journaling played an integral and new role. My wife and I used journaling to record notes and reflections and to survive the endless medical jargon, long doctor visits, and months away from

> **COURAGE IS NOT HAVING THE STRENGTH TO GO ON; IT'S GOING ON WHEN YOU DON'T HAVE THE STRENGTH.**
>
> — THEODORE ROOSEVELT

home. At the time, I did everything I could do to deal with the adversity positively, but it was not until a year later that I realized how much courage it takes to accept the anxiety of cancer, to acknowledge the unknown fear that comes along with it, and to just lean into what needs to be done. The courage to endure seemed like my only choice then, but upon deep reflection, I now know how lucky I really was for early detection, great doctors, and an incredible wife. I have found, over the years, that this personal journey has been important to share with others, knowing that it may, in some way, help them along a challenging journey someday.

ADVANTAGES OF JOURNALING

One of the benefits of journaling for more than two decades is that you get to create a lot of content about things that interest you. One of my favorite reflection activities is to occasionally take a dozen or so completed journals and see what topics dominated my thinking when I was recording them—sort of like opening up my own personal time capsule. I typically use legend categories (for example, Leadership) when I write in my journals. I've found, over the years, that certain topics become relevant and repeated across learnings, ideas, and connections.

As I focus in on specific leadership traits, this system of organizing thoughts helps me emphasize a compelling point of view on this topic. Sometimes, the answers exist within your own reflections, understandings, and notes, and this simple implementation for categorization can help you frame your perspective. Through my mentoring, I realized that one major goal of my journaling is to provide a solution for a problem presented by a mentee.

As I reflect on courageous moments of leadership throughout my career, I found observations recorded across a dozen journals that I would like to share with you.

The Origins of Courage to Lead

1. Early in my career, I had a boss who asked me what I thought he could do differently to become a better leader, and I thought to myself, "Wow, that took a lot of courage to ask!" I always remembered this and told myself, as a young professional, I hope I can do that someday if I'm ever lucky enough to become a boss. As my career expanded over time, I always remembered this lesson and looked for opportunities to do the same.

2. In my mid-career, I watched my manager publicly confront a toxic employee whose attitude was poisoning the team's culture and effectiveness. The intervention solved the challenge, and once again, I thought to myself—that took a lot of courage! I remembered a quote from an early journal that stated, "What you permit, you promote. What you allow, you encourage. What you condone, you own. [What you tolerate, you deserve.]" In other words, doing nothing actually validated the status quo of having a toxic employee as being acceptable. I knew, moving on, I needed the courage to do something.

3. At the end of my career, I was mentoring a lot, particularly a group of three young women who were making an incredible impact in their early careers and were committed to being even better. During the end of our sessions, I would always ask them to take a few minutes and teach back to me: a) what they observed, b) what they learned, and c) what they would commit to putting into action. Every call resulted in a very clear action plan. I thought that their desire to continuously ask for help, then wanting to put it into action to become better leaders, was courageous.

4. I was reviewing my journals one day and realized I recorded the same study in three different journals over a 10-year period on a book by Bonnie Ware, *The Top Five Regrets of the Dying*. Bonnie was a palliative nurse and collected the responses from people on their regrets in life. Number one was:

"I wish I had the courage to live a life true to myself, not the life others expected of me."

This regret really triggered me to deeply ruminate on why people do not have the courage to fulfill their ambitions and do what they were meant to do. I wanted to research this further.

5. Recently, the courage on the front lines during the COVID-19 pandemic showed an incredible strength from so many people, especially doctors and nurses. Their courage to help patients while putting their own lives at risk may be the greatest form of courage I have seen in my lifetime. We now need that same depth of courage as a nation to stand up for racial equality.

A COURAGEOUS REQUEST

A few years ago, I was asked by the superintendents of 25 local school systems in southern Wisconsin to conduct an educational session on leadership, courage, and the essential attributes high school seniors needed to focus on succeeding in college and in the world.

Luckily, I had been collecting material on the characteristics of courage and had already built some good material and key messages for the session. I was asked many great questions about leadership effectiveness.

This shifting perspective to younger generations, and the necessary courage for developing leaders, has brought new challenges and engaging conversations. In chapter 13, I answer many of the questions asked about leadership effectiveness during these sessions.

I also have been presenting many of the *Courage to Lead* components over the past decade in many forms, mainly in one-on-one coaching sessions with more than 50 global mentees.

The individuals and groups I work with are divergent, but the frustrations they face very often remain consistent. And they are the *same challenges* for leaders in all parts of the world.

I decided to become more rigorous in developing my own point of view of what courage in leadership, and life, really looks like. It quickly became apparent that the key points, or lessons, to develop courage in leadership can easily be adopted by those who want it.

This book was created to take the best learnings from the extensive treasure trove of journal content, share what I have learned, and provide others with a successful framework on how to be more courageous in their leadership endeavors while impacting the world even more.

THE IMPACT OF SOCIAL INJUSTICE AND SYSTEMIC RACISM

> "COURAGE IS NOT THE ABSENCE OF FEAR, BUT THE TRIUMPH OVER IT."
> - NELSON MANDELA

The tragic and unnecessary death of George Floyd in Minnesota spotlighted a serious problem that is 401 years overdue for transformational change and a permanent solution. The incredible unity of diverse Americans and communities across the globe, marching together will take incredible courage to make it a transformative and sustainable movement.

While significant changes are being seen already through this global movement against racial injustice, minority leaders who have stood up in the face of discrimination, brutality, exposure to COVID-19, and so many challenges faced daily by BIPOC (Black,

Indigenous, People of Color), while showing leadership, epitomizes **courage**.

It is now time for courageous leaders of all races, ethnicities, identities, and backgrounds to stand united, noticeably, and make their marks! Recent events have led my family and me to educate ourselves and get involved to make a difference. This ongoing conversation requires dedication to education from BIPOC perspectives, learning and relearning the whitewashed history of the United States. (See, for example, *A People's History of the United States,* by Howard Zinn.)

If you are interested in continuing this conversation about elevating BIPOC leaders and reaching differentially advantaged individuals for leadership training—please reach out to me directly at https://www.fourloop learning.com/contact/, as I firmly believe the art of deliberate reflection will help make a bigger impact.

> "ANGER IS THE PRELUDE TO COURAGE."
> - ERIC HOFFER

THE ORIGIN OF COURAGE

This is where the acronym COURAGE was created. It became more and more integral to expressing the rules of effective leadership. Many respected leaders fall short of greatness because they lack the one little internal nuance that "seals the deal." Cookie-cutter approaches weren't producing bigger and better results, particularly if they gave little thought to courage.

The complexities that create a courageous person regardless of one's position, are built over a lifetime of learnings. Becoming courageous requires Acknowledgement, Bolstered by practice, with Commitment to continuous improvement.

After studying leadership for more than 30 years at GE, and self-reflecting about it across 80 journals, I formalized "The COURAGE

The Origins of Courage to Lead

to Lead" as an integrated acronym for those who want to know more about the content.

These seven components on courage serve as a framework to help build more courageous leaders and connect directly to Hand, Heart & Head.

Change management as a core competency (✋)
Overcome mental chatter (🗣)
Use influence (🗣)
Relentlessly connect to people's hearts (♥)
Always look to improve (✋)
Get really good at implementation (✋)
Encourage iteration, not perfection (✋)

The rest of this book is a result of the insights from myriad mentoring sessions as well as the models that were created and refined to help leaders become more courageous. You hold in your hands the product from many years of helping shape improved leadership courage, from a comprehensive set of journals created over two decades.

My goal is that you can identify the skills to establish yourself as a courageous leader and then use these leadership skills courageously to make a difference in your world–regardless of scale, position, or background.

Taking the first step to acknowledge yourself as a leader is courageous. Every subsequent step to bettering yourself as a leader is courageous. I hope this book can direct you toward the courage within–and I hope you use the acronym COURAGE to promote innovation, learning, and dedication among those around you.

THE FIVE FUNDAMENTAL CHALLENGES

Certain principles of leadership are timeless. It's not hard to imagine, for instance, someone like George Washington or Joan of Arc bringing something to the table in the 21st century. The first thought of these two historical leaders brings to mind revolutionary stances and courageous actions, both of which were preserved through adversity.

> "THE BIGGEST HUMAN TEMPTATION IS TO SETTLE FOR TOO LITTLE."
> - THOMAS MERTON

Still, there is no denying that we face obstacles unique to, or heightened in, our era. Though the scope of these "tests" is wide indeed, I've narrowed them down to six fundamental challenges I found to be evident in my journal observations.

1. FEW LEADERS CAN LEAD COURAGEOUSLY

Here's the modern paradox. There is no particular shortage of leaders—or at least persons whose role or public persona is that of a leader. I would argue, however, that relatively few people truly demonstrate the courage to lead.

> "THE GREATER DANGER FOR MOST OF US LIES NOT IN SETTING OUR AIM TOO HIGH AND FALLING SHORT; BUT IN SETTING OUR AIM TOO LOW AND ACHIEVING OUR MARK."
>
> — **MICHELANGELO**

Why? Because of too few good role models to learn from as well as a real lack of confidence, frankly, in the leadership skills of the persons held up as "great."

The same names are brought up again and again. For example, innovators like Steve Jobs are frequently mentioned for generating incredible results but who also have a reputation for being harsh with people. Perhaps we can all find benefits in our day-to-day life from Steve Jobs' contributions as a leader—but consider how *you* would personally handle a brittle and consistently mean boss.

What can we do with that?

Furthermore, consider the lack of accountability—of owning an outcome—that is rampant in modern CEOs and other leaders. Everyone loves a winner, and everyone rushes to claim a winning idea, but we exist in an era where the buck stops *nowhere* after an unpopular decision.

Perhaps we can pinpoint the beginning of the accountability-drain to the mid-'80s. In the aftermath of the infamous "New Coke" debacle, wherein it was universally accepted that the company made a huge error in reformulating their classic soft drink. The company's CEO claimed to receive positive comments about the failed drink "at my country club." Meanwhile, a board member said he overhead praise about New Coke while on vacation at a resort in Mexico.

No one said, "My bad. Let's move on."

And do you remember all the CEOs and Chairpersons of the Board who came forward and apologized after the mortgage-loan debacle? Me neither.

The Five Fundamental Challenges

Now, fast forward many years.

It's awesome to see the new leaders making a big impact like activist Greta Thunberg who, at the inspiring age of 16, is tackling climate issues.

Greta has risen above the usual teenage qualms to tackle the challenge of her era. For many leaders, asserting courage for personal, professional, and global accountability is a daunting challenge. It may be easy to dismiss a daring, young Swedish environmentalist, but her perseverance and professionalism with political and world leaders is impressive. Environmentalists targeting corporations **demand** accountability.

Part of our objective is to help you think differently about building the skills and confidence to be a leader at any of the generational stages—one who has the courage to make big, bold, and positive changes in the things you believe in passionately.

Around the time I wrote this book, I asked one of my mentees how communications regarding the unnecessary George Floyd murder in Minnesota have been going. To my surprise, he said *only one of 300 managers* reached out to their employees for support. Devastated with his response, I decided to dedicate the remaining years of my life to help make a positive difference with journaling as the process to make a difference.

2. SPEED OF CHANGE CHALLENGES

I don't have to tell you the world is changing incredibly fast, with ongoing changes in economic indicators, life expectancy, and especially technology. I have *shoes* older than the smartphone, which has utterly transformed how the average person interacts with technology—i.e., a constant state of motion.

Four Loop Learning: Courage to Lead

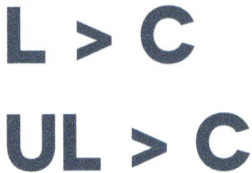

The illustration above depicts something I learned from Nick Binedell of the Gordon Institute of Business Science in Johannesburg, South Africa. Our only option in the face of such extraordinary speed of information growth is not only to LEARN faster than the speed of change but also to UNLEARN just as quickly.

People who remain tethered to old ideas and notions because they are comfortable (or because they passed a certification two years ago) are not going to succeed in a world where information travels, evolves, and grows at the speed of light.

Be nimble. Learn fast. *Unlearn* fast.

> **"THE ILLITERATE OF THE 21ST CENTURY WILL NOT BE THOSE WHO CANNOT READ AND WRITE, BUT THOSE WHO CANNOT LEARN, UNLEARN, AND RELEARN."**
> **- ALVIN TOFFLER**

It is another awakening to the VUCA World. In military parlance, that's **V**olatile, **U**ncertain, **C**omplex, and **A**mbiguous—certainly the ingredients that require a courageous leadership response. *(Note: In Africa, in the Zulu language, you'll find a similar word called "VUKA," which literally means "wake up!")*

Not too long ago, a manager or executive at a Fortune 500 company could be assured of a lifetime gig. After all, the lifespan of a Fortune 500 company was more than 50 years; plenty of time to get comfortable. If, however, you compare the Fortune 500 list in 1955 to the Fortune 500 in 2014, you will find only 61 companies on both lists.[1]

In 2013, America's top computer maker, Hewlett-Packard, was dumped from the Dow Jones Industrial Index, the list of 30 blue-chip stocks chosen to reflect the makeup of the U.S. economy. The same week, Bank of America and Alcoa also lost their spots. Even GE lost that distinction, which validates how difficult it is to be and stay in the top performing lists.

Consultant Richard N. Foster helped popularize the idea of "creative destruction," the process by which large companies get eliminated by the speed of change. He looked at the rate of "droppage" from the S&P 500—the 500 most valuable companies traded on the U.S. stock market—and found that the rate at which companies get eliminated from the S&P 500 has been accelerating. In 1958, 61 years was the span of time a company could expect to remain nested in the S&P 500.

Today, the average is just *18 years*.

Foster's idea—expressed in books like *Creative Destruction: Why Companies That Are Built to Last Underperform the Market—And How to Successfully Transform Them* and *Innovation: The Attacker's Advantage*—is that big companies are not able to somehow "out-innovate" the market. Foster believes that as well for entering new markets, which requires exceptionally bold and courageous leadership, to say the least.[2]

The average lifespan of a Fortune 500 Company has fallen to 16 years—so you better either lead boldly or have "what's next" plans.

Mull it over: How do millennials perceive this working world?

Let's look at the impact of knowledge availability and transfer.

Information is currently doubling every 13 months, which is already pretty astounding, but, according to IBM, the build-out of the "internet of things" and the industrial internet, where machines and sensors are connected to data, will lead to the doubling of knowledge every *12 hours*.[3]

Almost 4.57 billion people were active internet users as of July 2020, encompassing 59% of the global population.[4] By 2045, we expect ~*50 trillion* devices to be connected to the internet, giving and taking information.[5]

Think it's hard to keep up *now*?

That's just in *your* business. Now think about your workforce and colleagues. By 2025, 75% of the global workforce will be millennials (born between 1983 and 2004).[6]

Whether you are a member of this cohort or from a previous generation, adjustments consistent with this influx must be made—more on that later in Chapter Eleven: Example of Courage in Healthcare

THE COURAGE TO ACTUALLY TRANSFORM CHANGE

When Paul Polman was the CEO of Unilever, he took a very courageous stand to lead the company into the forefront of environmental and social responsibility. He instructed his leaders to stop focusing on quarterly results and make sure their sourcing practices were good for the *planet*, good for the *people*, and ultimately (if done responsibly) good for *profits* too. Under his courageous leadership, and as reported in their 2018 press release, 56% of the agricultural raw materials were sustainably sourced, which resulted in 12 brands having over one billion dollars in sales and validating that what's good for the planet can truly have a positive impact on profits. Alan Jope took over the CEO role in 2019. He shared his leadership beliefs on the courage to keep a good strategy alive.

"We believe that if we look after our employees and our customers, if we worry about society and the planet, if we take

care of our supplier partners, then our shareholders will be well rewarded." [7]

3. SUSTAINABLE LEADERSHIP

Often seen in schools through the perspective of educators, sustainable leadership plans for succession—for leaders within the school, and for students—as well as for lasting, meaningful improvements in learning.

Take a moment to reflect on the value of meaningful learning through your personal and professional experiences. Perhaps through journaling or conversations, the idea of sustainable growth as an individual, a company, or a community, is paramount to addressing and tackling necessary changes to reach success.

I said "success." Did you mean "money," or "meaningful change," or maybe "racial and social equity?" If one of the major components of sustainable leadership is reaching a determined long-term goal, it's crucial to define: a) **what** that goal is, b) **how** you can get there, and c) **what it takes**, as a leader, for you to make it happen.

This idea of sustainable leadership is often not seen in high-ranking positions from politics to corporate boardrooms. It's clear that capitalism breeds success by manipulating resources and often, by underpaying employees. So, what would compel a driven businessperson to adopt sustainable practices other than it seems like the *right* thing to do?

As a leader, adopting practices that emphasize impacts on people and the planet *as much as* profit requires courage. This framework and mindset are larger than using compostable tableware or supporting local farmers' markets. *(Although, both of these are great steps for reducing your carbon footprint.)* Sustainable leadership requires acknowledging environmental injustices which are deeply tied to racial and social injustices. Your boss may demand innovation and rapid turnaround on profits and success. Consider how long-term planning, and adopting diversity and inclusion practices, would *strengthen* the innovation and success through, let's say, an economic crisis and pandemic.

Are our current leaders teaching younger generations to become future leaders within the scope of climate change? I hope so. But this also falls on the shoulders of growing leaders to use innovation at the crossroads of science and business to create solutions.

I can't tell you what this looks like in your profession or how to achieve it through your dreams. The skills to be a sustainable and courageous leader, however, require learning, and plenty of unlearning and relearning, as well as a lifelong dedication to improve yourself, your community, and the world you live in.

4. VULNERABILITY AS THE KEY ESSENTIAL, BUT UNCOMFORTABLE, INGREDIENT

"Vulnerability" and "leadership" are not two words most people would say complement each other. Most leaders I have worked with say that being vulnerable is seen as a sign of weakness and to avoid it all cost. I asked one CEO what he meant by this, and he said, "Never let them see you sweat."

Dr. Brené Brown is an expert in understanding vulnerability. She defines vulnerability as uncertainty, risk, and emotional exposure. Her premise; there is no courage in leadership without vulnerability. Every time we fall, crash, and burn, it presents an opportunity to build some new muscle. I believe Brené really makes the point known when she says, "When you fall, get back up and begin again," as in each effort to claw yourself back, nothing is wasted, because the lessons are invaluable.

The Five Fundamental Challenges

I love to watch Brené on YouTube—and her advice on bouncing back during tough times was also reinforced during the commencement speech she did at the University of Texas.[8] "Your ability to live a life that's full of love and meaning, to make the world a braver and kinder place, to disrupt and reshape the future, has very little to do with the greatness of your plan. It depends completely on your ability to get back up and begin again when your plan fails.

One of the great quotes that also illustrates the point is from Theodore Roosevelt called "The Man in the Arena." He delivered the speech, entitled "Citizenship in a Republic," at the Sorbonne in Paris on April 23, 1910.

"It is not the critic who counts; not the man who points out how the strong man stumbles or where the doer of deeds could have done them better. The credit belongs to the man who is actually in the arena, whose face is marred by dust and sweat and blood; who strives valiantly; who errs, who comes short again and again, because there is no effort without error and shortcoming; but who does actually strive to do the deeds; who knows the great enthusiasms, the great devotions; who spends himself in a worthy cause; who at the best knows in the end the triumph of high achievement, and who at the worst, if he fails, at least fails while daring greatly, so that his place shall never be with those cold and timid souls who neither know victory nor defeat."

> **"IF YOU'RE GOING TO DARE GREATLY, YOU'RE GOING TO GET YOUR ASS KICKED AT SOME POINT. IF YOU CHOOSE COURAGE, YOU WILL ABSOLUTELY KNOW FAILURE, DISAPPOINTMENT, SETBACK, EVEN HEART-BREAK."**
> **- BRENÉ BROWN**

I also wanted to share that I had multiple journal entries highlighting my mentees, demonstrating a sincere vulnerability of how they were honestly doing. The benefit is that they gave me a true glimpse on the pulse of the organizational culture they work in.

5. NEED FOR AUTHENTIC INSPIRATION

John Quincy Adams was a member of multiple political parties over the years, serving as a diplomat, Senator, and member of the House of Representatives before becoming the sixth President of the United States. He stood against the expansion of slavery as enslaved people were arriving on the shore of the United States and helped to create some of the country's first foreign policy. As a son of President John Adams and Secretary of State to President Monroe, John Quincy Adams was deeply familiar with the early democracy's leadership, possessed the dedication required to constantly improve himself, and challenged those around him to be better leaders.

> "IF YOUR ACTIONS INSPIRE OTHERS TO DREAM MORE, DO MORE, AND BECOME MORE, YOU ARE A LEADER."
> - JOHN QUINCY ADAMS

One word in his quote jumps out immediately; INSPIRE. This word came up through Middle English as *inspiren*, derived from the Latin word *inspīrāre*, which means "to breathe upon or into."

Another component derived from the Latin roots of the word "inspiration" relates to the duality of generating harmony and diffusing tensions. As leaders, our goal is to inspire harmony (Inspira Concordia) and deflate the tensions.

INSPIRE

What are we doing when we lead, *besides* breathing life into a person or group of people? All impactful leadership has an element of inspiration. When I observe leaders in action, I determine if they are lifting their teams and breathing an air of encouragement into them or blowing them down with turbulent air currents.

The Five Fundamental Challenges

While there will always be situations where a tough message needs to be sent and teams need a reality check, most often, a positive approach is called for; one that usually yields a positive outcome. I've learned "you can catch more flies with honey than with vinegar" *(attributed to Benjamin Franklin)*. Below is a model based on my interpretation of what is required to be inspirational:

ELEMENTS OF INSPIRATION

$$\text{INSPIRATION} = f(P^4 + C + V + H)^B$$

WHERE
- P^4 = PEOPLE & PASSION > PROFITS & PROCESS
- C = CARE ABOUT YOUR PEOPLE – LOVE 'EM UP!
- V = VALUE GOOD & BAD NEWS WITH THE SAME INTENSITY
- H = HAVE THEIR BACKS – ESPECIALLY WITH FAILURE
- B = BE CONSISTENT

I also reviewed many of my journals and recorded what the best managers I worked for did, as well as who inspired me the most:

- They took the bullet for my mistakes and then taught me the lesson later, so I would remember not to repeat those mistakes.

- They provided very specific feedback on what I could do better and then continued to keep an eye on me *(i.e., a caring, non-intrusive approach)*.

- They cut me some slack when family medical issues needed tending to.

- They pushed me to be my best *and* to keep seeking ways to be more innovative and efficient while achieving greater results.

- They demonstrated courage in times of uncertainty.

- They also knew my wife's and children's names and made a special effort to remember milestones in my life (e.g., wishing me a happy birthday).

Managers who extend themselves in these ways compel extra discretionary effort. Employees feel appreciated and *want* to do an even *better* job!

THE SEVEN COMPONENTS OF COURAGE

It takes courage to unlearn and relearn, even when what you originally learned in the past was working and good enough to get by. This is a courageous acknowledgement in the self, to see perspectives outside of your own—drawn from different types and levels of education, background, and beliefs. Accepting the task of unlearning and relearning, the necessary step in re-educating yourself, takes time and often requires difficult realizations, or at least conversations.

The Courage to Lead is based upon seven attributes found in the acronym "COURAGE." In my assessment, leaders need to address these seven components of leadership. Doing so will allow them to understand the skills and reflection needed to be a courageous leader—with the potential to effect great change in a world that needs it.

> "COURAGE IS RESISTANCE TO FEAR, MASTERY OF FEAR, NOT THE ABSENCE OF FEAR."
>
> — MARK TWAIN

Change management as a core competency

Overcome mental chatter

Use influence

Relentlessly connect to people's hearts

Always look to improve

Get really good at implementation

Encourage iteration, not perfection

These seven components each came from a **challenge** that an individual or organization was facing and my subsequent **approach** to addressing that specific challenge.

I created a unique piecemeal solution to help them reflect upon, think through, and eventually develop a more impactful approach.

> "I CAN SHAKE OFF EVERYTHING IF I WRITE; MY SORROWS DISAPPEAR, MY COURAGE IS REBORN."
> - ANNE FRANK

A very enjoyable outcome would then occur. The discussion with my mentee or client would challenge the **dynamics** of the model—and after discussion of its advantages and shortcomings, the modified model would become even *better*.

This model continues to develop and grow through these ongoing conversations. Each mentee or individual may bring a similar problem, yet provide a unique focus for problem-solving, as well as a new perspective, which in turn helps me to create a more inclusive, and ultimately, more successful model.

4 CHANGE MANAGEMENT AS A CORE COMPETENCY

> "THE SECRET OF CHANGE IS TO FOCUS ALL OF YOUR ENERGY, NOT ON FIGHTING THE OLD, BUT ON BUILDING THE NEW."

THIS QUOTATION IS FROM A CHARACTER NAMED SOCRATES WHO WAS A GAS-STATION ATTENDANT IN WAY OF THE PEACEFUL WARRIOR (1980) BY DAN MILLMAN

Change Management as a Core Competency

COMMUNICATE THE MISSION, VISION, AND PURPOSE

Let's not beat around the bush—change is hard. The process of changing from the current state to the new creation of a desired state is challenging work.

Successful change management can be accelerated when others are involved in how the change is implemented.

> "CHANGE DONE TO ME IS DEBILITATING. CHANGE DONE WITH ME IS EXHILARATING."
> - JOHN BUCKLEY
> —US ARMY

Another important component of change is how to proactively address the population of employees who will be averse to change, seeing disruptions to the status quo as harmful.

The following quote from Martin Luther King provides a great example of how to address this population effectively with courage.

> *"We must build dikes of courage to hold back the flood of fear."*
>
> —Martin Luther King

People and organizations fall into comfortable patterns, and it becomes very disruptive to even *mention* the notion of making big or small changes. Confidence is built by comfort in a "well-worn groove"—and who wants their confidence shaken?

You want people to feel they have "skin in the game." To overcome apprehensions, they need to feel energized about being a part of the overall effort.

In their book, *Switch: How to Change Things When Change is Hard*, co-authors Chip and Dan Heath cite University of Virginia Psychologist Jonathan Haidt's suggestion that to make true change, effective leaders need to recognize the duality in individuals. In their model this consists of the Elephant, which is our Emotional side, and the Rider, which is our Rational persona.[9]

Ostensibly, the Rider has the reins and is in charge of the Elephant. The Rider, however, can hardly be expected to control a six-ton Elephant when the two have a difference in opinion over which way to go. The Elephant is what makes you eat that gallon of ice cream even when you know that you want to lose 15 pounds. The rational Rider steered you away; the powerful Elephant got out the ice cream scoop, anyway.

The Elephant is about short-term gratification; the Rider is long-term thinking. So, the Rider is always the most valuable component of our psyche, correct?

Wrong! The Elephant is all emotion—loyalty, sympathy, anger, love—the things that spur heroic acts in the face of ridiculous odds. When a person rushes to a burning vehicle to save the driver, that's the Elephant ignoring the reins of the Rider, who would have thought rationally about the risks and ran sensibly the other way.

The Rider is also the over-analyzer and over thinker. If you've been across the table from a person who can't lift his or her head from the menu because the choice between traditional fries or curly fries was just too daunting, you've experienced someone with a Rider malfunction.

The Elephant is energy and drive; it gets things done and motivates movement. You aren't going to affect actual change without appealing to the Elephant. In addition to that energy, however, you need the planning and direction of the Rider.

Head (🧠) *and* heart (♥). *That's* what puts "skin in the game."

As a courageous leader, you must allow everyone to have their *say*, but not everyone can have their *way*. That means your appeal

Change Management as a Core Competency

to the Elephant—the positive emotional response that comes from "winning" the point—must be countered by an equally strong or stronger Rational appeal to the Rider.

In my 30 years of learning about change management, the most valuable player has and continues to be the marketing communications expert. Winning over the Elephant *and* the Rider can only happen with effective delivery of your message.

Think I'm leaning too hard on communication? Let's take a look, through these landmark studies, at the leading reasons change does not "stick."

CHANGE MANAGEMENT
TURNING GREAT STRATEGY INTO GREAT PERFORMANCE
MICHAEL C MANKINS & RICHARD STEELE

- **5.2% POORLY COMMUNICATED STRATEGY**
- 4.5% ACTIONS REQUIRED TO EXECUTE ARE NOT CLEAR
- 4.1% UNCLEAR ACCOUNTABILITIES FOR EXECUTION
- 3.7% ORGANIZATIONAL SILOS AND CULTURE IS BLOCKING EXECUTION
- 3.0% INADEQUATE PERFORMANCE MONITORING

Source: Marakon Associates, in collaboration with the Economist Intelligence Unit, Fall 2004 [10]

Four Loop Learning: Courage to Lead

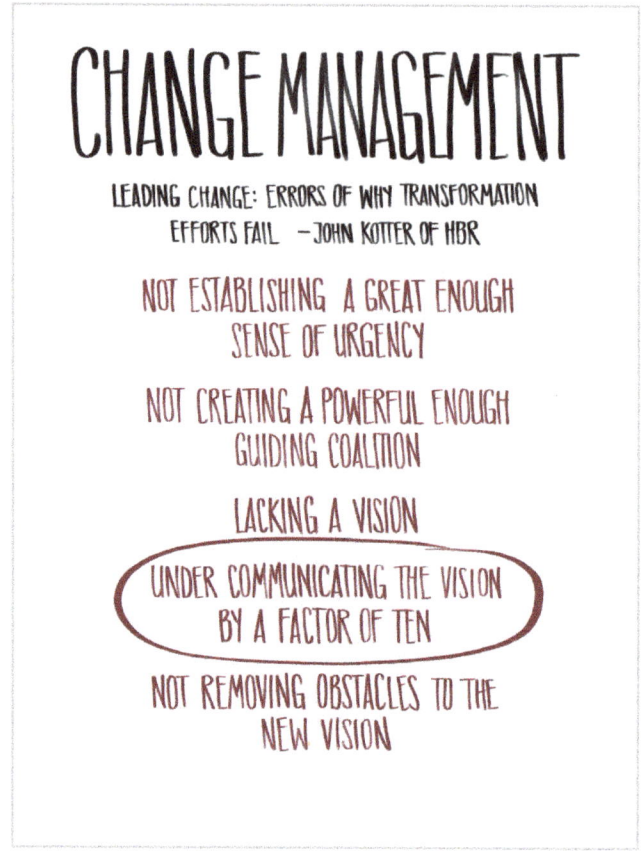

Source: John P. Kotter, Harvard Business Review, May-June 1995 [11]

The common thread? **Poor communication.** Perhaps the Rider was well addressed with facts and figures, but there wasn't much to offer the Elephant in terms of illustrating positive personal stakes in the change. An extra ingredient is needed.

How does a leader address this hurdle? Consider the findings of Dr. Albert Mehrabian of UCLA. When people are exposed to an idea one time, they retain 10% or less of it after 30 days. However, when people are exposed to the same idea six times, with *interval reinforcement*, their retention is 90% at the end of 30 days. [12]

You also have to be cognizant of the impact body language has on the message. Mehrabian is also known for this rule; 7% of what we communicate consists of the literal content of the message. The use of one's voice, such as tone, intonation and volume, take up 38%, and as much as 55% of communication consists of body language.

From a practical standpoint, this enforces the notion that big, onetime splash extravaganzas should be replaced with a series of connected and coordinated messaging events.

Share the strategy—what's in it for the customer and the employee—in a very collaborative and connected way at least **six separate times**. It takes courage to do this. I found that most CEOs do not like repeating the same message, yet the research shows how beneficial it can be.

I once saw an executive start a town hall meeting asking everyone why they thought he was there. He addressed some responses for about five minutes and then asked again, "Why do you think I am here?" The same process repeated itself for another five minutes, and then he asked a third time. At this point, he had everyone's attention and told them the heartfelt and authentic reason—and I bet all 200 people in the room would never forget what was said.

FIND AND LEVERAGE THE INFLUENCERS

Many times, it also comes down to *who* is doing the change.

You might be tempted to turn to individuals you identify as innovators to help send your message. It turns out that's exactly *wrong*. In the book *Influencer: The New Science of Leading Change* (2013)[13], Joseph Grenny and Kerry Patterson say innovators are exactly who you want to *avoid* in the quest to spread change. Instead, they cite Dr. Everett Rogers' findings; the ability for an innovation to be adopted is determined by whether or not early adopters or *opinion leaders* adopt the idea.

Learn to identify and target the opinion leaders in your organization or group. About 13.5% of any given organization's population are the opinion leaders—the true influencers—in that group. They are the persons you ask, "What is going on?"

According to Rogers, "The rest of the population—over 85%—will not adopt the new practices *until opinion leaders do.*"[14]

It can seem that the people with the power and influence to make change are missing when the collaborative conversations based around growth and innovation are happening.

Once you find out who these people are, arm them with information as to why change is needed. They have access to the Elephant in ways a PowerPoint presentation cannot hope to provide. This is where I learned the expression "it's the power of the point, not the PowerPoint."

In other words, seek a **full connection** to the importance of communication.

HAVE THE COURAGE TO STOP AND REFLECT

One of the big lessons I learned is how difficult it is to stop and reflect on what you are doing when things are going well. The speed of disruption is so daunting that resting on your laurels, and not moving faster than the speed of the market, is a sign of early death.

As you stand still, thousands of people are trying to figure out how to disrupt your business model and grab a piece of the profits. The most courageous leaders constantly give themselves time to think deeply about the current state of their people, processes, and marketplace offerings so they can stay ahead of the learning curve.

My first book on _Four Loop Learning: The Art of Journaling and Leadership Reflection_ uses a process called **Stop & Reflect**, where you review the contents of the past 50 pages and re-record the most important or relevant learnings.

The next step is to _narrow down_ all those valuable lessons to the _one_ most important thing that you will commit to act upon, to become a higher impact leader.

KEY RESOURCE:

I've created a customized leadership reflections journal to formalize the Stop & Reflect feature, as well as explain the benefits of the four loops of learning, which are to Record, Reflect, Act, and Share. More information is available on my website, www.FourLoopLearning.com.

5
OVERCOME MENTAL CHATTER

> "IF YOU HEAR A VOICE WITHIN YOU SAY, 'YOU CANNOT PAINT,' THEN BY ALL MEANS PAINT, AND THAT VOICE WILL BE SILENCED."
>
> — VINCENT VAN GOGH

Overcome Mental Chatter

Overcome Mental Chatter

Let's talk about the voices in your head.

We all have them. Some of us hear them more than others. Some of us are affected by them more than others. Whether to a greater or smaller degree, no one can deny the effect of "mental chatter."

> "THE INNER SPEECH, YOUR THOUGHTS, CAN CAUSE YOU TO BE RICH OR POOR, LOVED OR UNLOVED, HAPPY OR UNHAPPY, ATTRACTIVE OR UNATTRACTIVE, POWERFUL OR WEAK."
> - RALPH CHARELL

So no question that having some control over that mental chatter—keeping positive and free from anxiety—is vital to overcoming obstacles.

This is easier said than done, of course. All the possible bad consequences or shortfalls ahead are just too clear when contemplating a "leap." Our minds are well-tuned to simulate catastrophes, no matter how far-fetched.

Here are some strategies to tame your mental chatter and increase your courage.

PREPARE LIKE ALEXANDRA

Alexandra Kosteniuk is a Russian chess grandmaster and a former Women's World Chess Champion. She was a member of the Russian team at the Women's Chess Olympiads of 2010, 2012 and 2014, winning Gold in each instance. She also competed at the Women's European Team Chess Championships of 2007, 2009, 2011, 2015, and 2017.

If you've read Malcolm Gladwell's work in his book, *Outliers: The Story of Success* (2008), you'll know that he famously stated the "10,000-hour rule" as the path to expertise. In other words, to become a great guitar player or surfer, for example, one must apply 10,000 hours of practice to the skill.

Four Loop Learning: Courage to Lead

Gladwell noted that the 10,000-hour rule applied to becoming an expert at chess. Consider this: A Grandmaster is two times better than a Master, and a Master is ten times better than an expert. So mathematically speaking, Alexandra Kosteniuk needed 200,000 hours of practice to become a Grandmaster.

200,000 hours is 22.82 *years*–24 hours a day. Ms. Kosteniuk was awarded the status of Women's Grandmaster at age 14 and International Grandmaster in 2004 when she was 20 years old.

Gladwell's "10,000-hour rule," of course, has been the victim of oversimplification. In *Outliers*, Gladwell *actually* wrote "achievement is talent plus preparation." But he also elaborated, "…The closer psychologists look at the careers of the gifted, the smaller the role innate talent seems to play, and the bigger the role preparation seems to play." [15]

For Alexandra, her talent was **recognizing patterns**. She was taught to play chess at the age of five by her father and capitalized on her innate ability by studying chess combinations and patterns constantly and regularly. At the age of seven, she was setting up a board on the sidewalk in Moscow, beating all comers.

Alexandra, in her childhood as "chess hustler."
(Source: Alexandra Kosteniuk blog, crediting Stein in Oslo, Norway) [16]

To attain and maintain mastery without having to practice 24 hours a day for two decades, Alexandra maintained a standard practice of routinely and regularly studying the patterns of the game. This level of preparation—coupled with regular and habitual practice—made her confident that she'd recognize virtually any combination or pattern she was likely to encounter, or learn the ones she'd missed in the near future. Her mental chatter had no room for pessimistic thoughts.

Courageous leaders also concentrate on learning and seeing the patterns, and then they do the right thing for maximum impact. Being in a constant and regular learning state creates the confidence needed to know that, despite the accelerated rate of change and information growth we currently face, we possess the tools needed to see the path through. **Journaling** is a way to allow your brain to reach a regular state of learning through daily thought-provoking ideas and reflections.

When you create a habit of ongoing learning, you won't worry about today's pattern becoming tomorrow's maze—you are set up to move from one paradigm to the next.

READ AND RUN LIKE WILL

A generation of people now entering the workforce may have heard the words of Will Smith as he accepted a statuette at the Nickelodeon Awards:

"The keys to life are running and reading. Why running? When you're running, there's a little person that talks to you and says, 'Oh, I'm tired. My lung's about to pop. I'm so hurt. There's no way I can possibly continue.' And you want to quit, right? If you learn how to defeat that person when you're running, you will learn how to not quit when things get hard in your life.

"For reading: there have been millions and millions and gazillions of people that have lived before all of us. There's no new problem you could have—with your parents, with school, with a bully, with anything. There's no new problem that someone hasn't already solved and wrote about it in a book.

"So, the keys to life are running and reading." [17]

Granted, Will Smith was tailoring his statement for a preteen audience, but in his simplification, Smith hit upon a nice set of metaphors that can help us with the challenge of overcoming mental chatter. Defeat the "little person's" argument during challenging instances like a long run, and you are bound to create a habit of recognizing that little person when he or she tells you that, for instance, learning a new language is too hard.

You beat that person before, remember?

It also pays to realize that the store of knowledge that exists around you—completely accessible as needed—could very well address any problem or challenge you might encounter. Draw upon the experience of people who have been "down the road" before you.

And if you have truly found a new road, **be** *the person to write the book!*

LESSONS FROM DAVID

In 2015, I had the distinct honor and pleasure to give a presentation at the [Galleria Dell'Accademia di Firenze](#) in Florence, Italy beneath Michelangelo's amazing statue of David. What a unique and humbling experience. The "mind chatter" I experienced had to do with wondering what significant contributions I could make in my life as a leader or in my practice of "sculpting" the impact of courageous leadership with people. It was a great way to energize myself instead of letting the thoughts minimize me.

David stands 17 feet tall, and it's carved from a two-ton chunk of white Carrara marble. It was originally commissioned to be one of a series of statues of prophets positioned along the roofline of the Santa Maria del Fiore Cathedral, but it was unveiled as the biblical hero David and his sling—after quite a journey to completion.

The work was first commissioned to the Florentine sculptor Agostino di Duccio in 1464, who actually got started carving the block of marble. [18]

Three years later, Agostino was taken off the project for reasons unknown. (Some say both he and his successor, Antonio Rossellino, complained of the presence of too many "*taroli*," or imperfections, which could threaten the stability of such a huge statue.) In 1475, Rossellino was commissioned to finish the project. His contract was terminated soon afterward. The block of marble sat in the yard of the cathedral workshop—fully exposed to the elements—for 25 years.

It was an expensive piece of marble, transported at great cost to Florence, so cathedral authorities were anxious to find a way to use it. They gathered input from everyone who was anyone in the art world. (In fact, Leonardo da Vinci was consulted.)

Finally, 26-year-old Michelangelo—already one of the era's star artists—convinced the cathedral powers that he was the man for the job.

It is said the sculptor created a wax model of his design and submerged it in a tank of water. As he worked, he let the water level drop, and sculpted what was revealed—an intriguing approach to taming what could appear to most people an utterly overwhelming project. After a little more than two years of work, Michelangelo presented the sculpture to the members of the Vestry Board and to Pier Soderini, the *gonfaloniere* of the Republic. It took four days and 40 men to move the statue the half-mile distance from Michelangelo's workshop behind Santa Maria del Fiore Cathedral to the Piazza della Signoria. It was unveiled in January 1504 to great acclaim.

Beyond the statue's visual majesty and masterful execution, it is amazing for the moment Michelangelo chose to depict. Other classic statues and paintings of David in this period show him after victory over the giant Goliath, most often with his foot upon the severed head of his vanquished foe. Michelangelo's David appears to depict the hero in the moments after he made the decision to fight Goliath, but before the battle has actually begun—that instance between conscious choice and confident action. His eyes glow with steely, yet calm, resolve. His body is at ease in the classic pose called *contrapposto* (counterpoise).

You can imagine David when contemplating what it looks like to have your mental chatter overcome and your focus complete. The various combinations have been weighed; the alternatives examined and discarded; standard practices in constant learning have done their job in updating what choices are possible; the inner voice of negativity and fear has been squelched.

The giant doesn't stand a chance.

And you *know* it. This is what a courageous leader looks like moments before action.

REPLACE GUILT WITH HOPE

One of my mentees, an exceptional leader who energizes her team and delivers great results, recently shared that she had to take time off to address a family challenge and felt guilty she was absent from her work.

First, I shared my admiration that she focused on her family as the most important priority. I then composed the following acronym, to provide her with a more courageous way to think about it:

> "EVERY BLOCK OF STONE HAS A STATUE INSIDE IT, AND IT IS THE TASK OF THE SCULPTOR TO DISCOVER IT. I SAW THE ANGEL IN THE MARBLE AND CARVED UNTIL I SET HIM FREE ... THE GREATEST ARTIST HAS NO CONCEPTION WHICH A SINGLE BLOCK OF MARBLE DOES NOT POTENTIALLY CONTAIN WITHIN ITS MASS— BUT ONLY A HAND OBEDIENT TO THE MIND CAN PENETRATE TO THIS IMAGE."
>
> - MICHELANGELO[19]

Replace GUILT with HOPE, where:

GUILT = **G**oing to **U**ncouple **I**ncomplete and **L**imited **T**hinking, with

HOPE = **H**aving **O**nly **P**ositive **E**xpectations

She printed this on a notecard which hangs in her office as a constant reminder not to let her negative chatter get the best of her.

6 USE INFLUENCE

> "REAL POWER HAS TO DO WITH ONE'S ABILITY TO INFLUENCE THE HEARTS AND MINDS OF OTHERS."[20]
>
> — DALAI LAMA

Four Loop Learning: Courage to Lead

Use Influence

Use Influence

SOMETHING GREAT RULE

WHAT IS SOMETHING GREAT THAT HAS HAPPENED TO YOU IN THE PAST 24 HOURS?

When I present in front of groups, I like to start by asking attendees to think about something great that has happened to them in the past 24 hours. I then ask them to share that great thing with the person next to them for about five minutes.

Naturally, what happens is everybody is very excited to share something great that has happened in his or her life—the energy in the room notches up and the volume increases as attendees unspool their stories.

I then pull everybody back together and ask them, "*Why* would I want to start off a meeting asking you to tell me something good that's happened to you in the past 24 hours?"

> "NEVER UNDERESTIMATE THE INFLUENCE YOU HAVE ON OTHERS."
> - LAURIE BUCHANAN

The reason: it's all about **setting the mood**. Do you want to start a meeting with energy and positivity—"What's something great that you experienced in the past 24 hours?"—or do you want to be the bearer of bad news right out of the gate?

Every day as a leader, you make that courageous choice. What kind of mood am I going to set for my organization?

MOOD^3

Four Loop Learning: Courage to Lead

I'm constantly asked, for example, how to set the right mood based upon the uniqueness of each leadership situation. In response, I share a model I created called Mood to the third power, where we recognize three different moods that leaders need to be aware of in order to drive effective change.

FIRST is *their* mood and to be cognizant of it.

SECOND is the mood of the people they are *with*.

THIRD—and most importantly—is the mood that needs to be carefully *created* and *deliberately set or adjusted* to have the best possible chance of a positive outcome.

Simply put, ask three questions about yourself and your colleagues:

1. What is your current mood?

2. What is the mood of the people in the room? Engaged? Arms crossed? Angry?

3. Knowing the above, as the "conductor of the music" that will happen, working together, how do you set or adjust the mood for optimal impact?

That sounds easy, right? It turns out, though, that most people I work with are not even aware of the third mood, because frankly, they don't have the confidence or courage to look beyond themselves.

Getting "outside oneself," we can agree, requires some guts! In my experience, only 5% of the leaders I work with deliberately set the optimal mood, so this is a bit more difficult than it appears.

I was amazed to see how many times a leader was in a bad mood and did not even seem to know it! I created the following model from multiple journal entries on what an undetected Bad Mood can do to a team's performance.

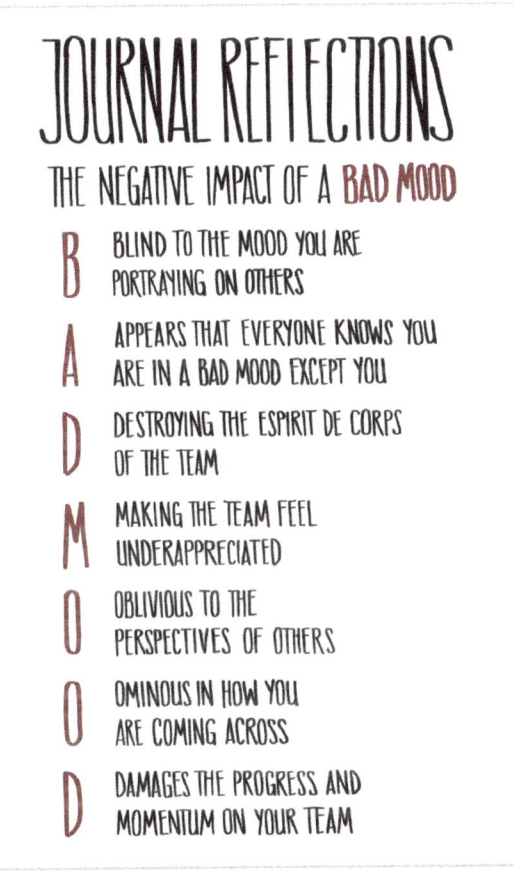

A MANAGER'S IMPACT ON ENGAGEMENT

70 – 57–1

70

"Research shows that a manager has a tremendous amount of impact on an employee's level of commitment. In fact, more than

70% of an employee's commitment is based upon the manager's interaction."[21]

57

"Engaged employees can yield up to **57%** more discretionary effort."[22]

1

"The number **1** reason people leave a company is their immediate manager."[23]

Do you have a great opportunity that is going to require an extra push from your team? They're much more likely to roll up their sleeves and dive in when they sense that their immediate manager is on their side, supporting their efforts, and going to bat for them time and time again in a supportive way.

Leaders need to inspire their teams to do great work, learn from failures, and always offer an open path to trying new ideas and approaches. This is why the Inspiration model in Chapter 2 is so important. Inspiring your employees is one of the most important activities a leader does.

Every morning, as a courageous leader, you have to consciously decide to live on the **green** side of this equation, or get **red**-y to *risk* feeding a stream of resumes to job sites, Glassdoor, etc., from persons looking to get away from *you*.

People don't leave organizations. They leave *managers*.

7
RELENTLESSLY CONNECT TO PEOPLE'S HEARTS (♥)

"PEOPLE WILL WORK HARD FOR MONEY. THEY WILL WORK HARDER FOR OTHERS. BUT THEY WILL WORK HARDEST OF ALL WHEN THEY ARE DEDICATED TO A CAUSE."

HARRY EMERSON FOSDICK

Four Loop Learning: Courage to Lead

Relentlessly Connect to People's Hearts

STRIVE FOR PURPOSE

If you are going to be a leader, it's important to understand why people get up out of bed in the morning and want to work for an organization—not to mention why they want to make a positive impact in the world and on mankind in general.

> "THE PURPOSE OF LIFE IS TO DISCOVER YOUR GIFT. THE WORK OF LIFE IS TO DEVELOP IT. THE MEANING OF LIFE IS TO GIVE YOUR GIFT AWAY."
> - DAVID S. VISCOTT

A 2016 study by Claudine Gartenberg suggests a positive impact on both operating financial performance (i.e., return on assets) and forward-looking measures (i.e., stock returns) when an organization's purpose is communicated with clarity. [24]

When Alan Jope took over the CEO role at Unilever, he reinforced the focus of the preceding CEO Paul Polman that the company had three deeply held beliefs: "that brands with purpose grow, companies with purpose last, and people with purpose thrive. [25]

One of the most powerful tools in an organization—and one that should be given serious consideration in its development and promotion within an organization—is the **Purpose Statement.**

It was coined as the new management watchword in 2010, is the heartbeat of a company, and according to Harvard, it's the foundation for creating the vision, executing on the mission, and abiding by the values. [26]

Why are Purpose Statements so important?

1. Purpose Statements are encapsulations of your organization's reason for being.
2. Having a strong Purpose Statement helps inspire employees, motivates teams, and aligns the organization to a common vision.
3. Tactically, it helps each level of the organization prioritize work, weeding out the urgent from the strategic.

A strong, clearly stated Purpose Statement also helps develop sharper marketing messages when communicating your value to potential customers or users.

It's the *reinforcement of a strong organizational community ethic*, however, that we're most concerned with as leaders.

An exercise recommended by the folks who create the great Guerrilla Marketing books is to write three sentences that describe your organization.

1. Why does your organization exist?   (Make sure you talk about your **passions**.)
2. What does your organization do?   (Talk about what you're **best** at.)
3. What difference does it make?   (What **impact** is your organization making?)[27]

From the answers, you should be able to construct a Purpose Statement that either explicitly or implicitly addresses each of those questions.

Let's look at a few really good Purpose Statements.

EXAMPLES OF SOME OF MY FAVORITE PURPOSE STATEMENTS

Google–To organize the world's information and make it universally accessible and useful.

Nike–To inspire the athlete in all of us.

Starbucks–To nurture the human spirit.

Coca-Cola–To refresh the world with moments of optimism and happiness.

Khan Academy–To provide a free world-class education for anyone anywhere.

Harvard Business School–To improve the practice of management and its impact on the changing world.

Zappos.com–To provide the best customer service possible.

GE Aviation–Reinvent the future of flight, lift people up, and bring them home safely.

IAG–To help people manage risk and recover from the hardship of unexpected loss.

Kellogg–Nourishing families so they can flourish and thrive.

Twitter–To give everyone the power to create and share ideas and information instantly, without barriers.

Whole Foods–With great courage, integrity and love—we embrace our responsibility to co-create a world where each of us, our communities, and our planet can flourish. All the while, celebrating the sheer love and joy of food.

The employees of the organizations above—from CEO down to interns—need not wade through a 100-page employee handbook to learn what their primary focus should be.

Note that the Purpose Statements are *outwardly focused*. They don't say things like, "To concentrate on accomplishing my sectional goals so our project group will get an 'A' rating at quarterly reviews."

Google's Purpose Statement sounds simple, but it actually clarifies the company's mission beautifully. A few years ago, when Larry Page took an entire day driving around Palo Alto with a small handheld camera—driving for a few feet and then stopping to take a few pictures—he did so confidently. The massive project that became the now-familiar Street View available on Google Maps, mapping every street in the world, was right in line with "organizing the world's information and making it universally accessible and useful."[28]

Every employee and manager involved in that prodigious, almost impossible-sounding effort (visually map *every* street, road, and highway in the world?) could confidently embrace it. This large scale accomplishment *never* could have been attempted without complete buy-in from everyone involved—because they knew they were working for a clearly stated purpose.

Page's acquisition and development of Android also remained true to Google's Purpose Statement. The Android platform helped proliferate handheld connected computing devices in a way the iPhone alone could not. More people had access to information—and to Google's revenue-creating ad platform.

Google's Purpose Statement also informed Page's decision to return as CEO of the company after 10 years of working in the background. While the CEO chosen by Google's investors had done a great job keeping the company profitable, Page sensed they were no longer making the great leaps of innovation that should be possible with Google's resources and talents. During a product pitch by one of his executives, Page suddenly interrupted by saying, "No—we don't do this. We build products that leverage technology to solve huge problems for hundreds of millions of people. Look at Android. Look at Gmail. Look at Google Maps. Look at Google Search. That's what we do. We build products you can't live without. This is not it."

Relentlessly Connect to People's Hearts

He did not need to explain further. Google's Purpose Statement—"To organize the world's information and make it universally accessible and useful"—perfectly instilled the company's goals.

Create purpose and you will create partners. Create partners and you will create anything your team can imagine.

NEW ORGANIZATIONAL FOCUS ON PURPOSE

One of the best examples of courage happened in August 2019, when 181 high-ranking executives pledged to abandon a shareholder and profit strategy for a new approach that benefits employees, customers, investors, and society at large.[29]

The members of the Business Roundtable, led by Jamie Dimon, Chairman and CEO of JPMorgan Chase & Co. and Chairman of Business Roundtable, created a new Statement on the Purpose of a Corporation with five core commitments that each company fundamentally shared:

1. Delivering value to our customers
2. Investing in our employees
3. Dealing fairly and ethically with suppliers
4. Supporting communities
5. Generating long-term value for shareholders

It takes a lot of courage to adopt these five commitments when the focus has been on profits and financial measures for the last 200 years.

T-SHIRT WITH A PURPOSE

One of the exercises I conducted with my team and mentees is called the Forward-Thinking T-shirt exercise. I asked them to ruminate about their retirement date, and to then visualize (if they were being presented with a T-shirt that summed up their career) what that T-shirt would say.

For example, I once asked a team member what they thought the T-shirt would say about a peer, and the answer was, "They duck and stay for peace and pay." I responded that if that person keeps on doing what they are currently doing, with no evidence of change, they will have a very challenging career. If I were mentoring that individual, I would encourage him or her to aspire for a T-shirt that says, "I love what I do, and it shows," and then identify the daily behaviors that would make the T-shirt come true.

8
ALWAYS LOOK TO IMPROVE

> **"IMPROVEMENT IS BETTER THAN DELAYED PERFECTION."**
>
> — MARK TWAIN

Four Loop Learning: Courage to Lead

A
ALWAYS LOOK TO IMPROVE

BENCHMARK THE TOP COMPANIES
TOP COMPANIES FOR LEADERSHIP

One of the best ways to evaluate current Leadership best practices is to benchmark what the top leadership development organizations are doing for their employees.

Companies like Korn Ferry/Hay Group, Aon Hewett, Deloitte, McKinsey and Bain (to name a few) conduct comprehensive studies and then position their strengths to the leadership development opportunities they uncover.

Here are four disciplines from the Hay Group study that differentiate the top companies:

1. For more than a decade, the Aon Hewett Top Companies for Leaders® research shows what separates top companies from other participating organizations.[30]

The study also highlighted three key attributes of the leadership mindset required in today's uncertain environment.

ENGAGING LEADERSHIP

Leaders infuse their teams with purpose, commitment, and authenticity.

RESILIENCE

Leaders take risks, fail fast, learn, and then adapt to win.

SELF-AWARENESS

Leaders reflect on their own behaviors and modify their actions that affect the outcomes of their colleagues.

The primary causes of derailment in executives involve deficits in emotional competence. What exactly is emotional competence? Basically, the ability to be self-aware.

The top three "executive derailers" relate to Self-Awareness:

1. Difficulty in handling change
2. Not being able to work well in a team
3. Poor interpersonal relations[31]

One thing is clear. The best companies are absolutely committed to developing leaders—in both good *and* bad economic times, with *no time off* from developing talent and leaders.

SELF-AWARENESS NOW INCLUDES CLIMATE CHANGE AND RACIAL JUSTICE

What is an **externality**? It's a fancy economic term for a side effect or consequence of an industrial or commercial activity that affects other parties *without* this being reflected in the cost of the goods or services involved.

This concept extends at least as far back as Garrett Hardins' presentation on December 13, 1968, in which he discussed the "tragedy of the commons," a situation in a shared-resource system where individual users, acting independently according to their own self-interest, behave contrary to the common good of all users by depleting or spoiling the shared resource through their collective action.

For example, it is widely known that a small percentage of large corporations are responsible for outsized contributions to global climate change. In fact, recent reports state that just 100 energy companies have been responsible for 71% of all industrial emissions since human-driven climate change was officially recognized.[32]

Now we are seeing big corporations like Delta Air Lines and BP[33] promising to go carbon neutral, making lofty promises on climate goals. As the world creeps closer and closer to the red lines drawn repeatedly by climate scientists, these goals to halt or reverse carbon emissions become increasingly important.

Many large corporations are considering climate change as a corporate social responsibility issue. This is logical, in that climate-change policies will influence stakeholders and thus shape a company's perspective for social responsibility.

This categorization, however, is dangerous. If climate change is not considered a **business** problem, corporations functioning on financial deadlines will never truly implement progressive practices to tackle climate change, because it just doesn't mesh well with the bottom line or capitalism.

In reading this, you may say, "But I'm just one person—I'll lose my job if I can't bring in the right amount of money this quarter" *(or words to that effect)*. These short-term perspectives, requiring quick turnarounds, rapid results, and explosive financial gain, seriously threaten establishing any worthwhile and useful climate-change prevention plans.

Soon, carbon emissions will be expensive for business leaders. Companies will be vulnerable to climate-related environmental and economic shocks[34]. Many components of climate-related problems could influence your job and your company. How would *your* company proceed without accessible energy, water, or infrastructure? How has *your* company handled the crash of the economy amidst a pandemic?

It is paramount that leaders **reframe** the challenges of climate change to address responsibility on a corporate level while also acknowledging that *environmental* justice is deeply tied to *racial* justice.

Soon, if they aren't already, leaders will weigh their current role against how climate change will influence their companies' future competition. Companies including Microsoft and Google are investing in renewable energy resources to meet carbon emission reduction targets. A new Environmental Defense Fund report found that "92% of business leaders believe emerging technologies can boost ROI and sustainability–yet only 59% of executives are making investments in these technologies."[35]

Consider this interesting paradox; a company may implement sustainable measures to increase their profits and look progressive in the eyes of the consumers while actually making *no* progress toward climate goals–or perhaps, even *worsening* progress toward these goals.

With all of these new considerations to account for, how can executives possibly exhibit the courage to lead in these trying times? For starters, by being more mindful about, and then action-oriented in response to, potential derailers.

MITIGATE AGAINST THE DERAILERS

In my experiences throughout the globe, I have personally seen the following six derailers in leaders worldwide:

1. They are not self-aware and constantly lead with multiple emotional intelligence dysfunctionalities; e.g., cutting people off, rolling their eyes at ideas, and trying to multitask in the middle of important conversations.
2. They no longer value dissent from their teams, and "devil's advocate" points of view are no longer requested.
3. They maniacally drive process over purpose and lose the heartfelt connections with the employees who are working so hard for them.
4. They surround themselves with people just like them, which immediately kills diverse points of view. I refer to this as a "team of same is a team of lame."
5. They are not learning at the speed of change of their customers and industry, and they are not courageous enough to Unlearn and Relearn.
6. They are just not able to give up control.

WHAT IF I HAD IT AND THEN I LOSE IT?

Below is a collection on the 12 ways a leader can have it and then LOSE it.

I'm a big advocate of using ratios as a metaphor for coaching to help unlock potential.

To make sure that you continue to HAVE it and not LOSE it, I share four situational ratios that spell STOP. *(Note: These are metaphors for making a point and are not true mathematical expressions.)*

Four Loop Learning: Courage to Lead

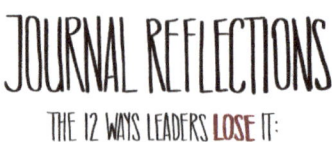

JOURNAL REFLECTIONS
THE 12 WAYS LEADERS LOSE IT:

L
- LOST TOUCH
- LIMITED VIEW OF REALITY
- LEAD WITH COMPLACENCY

O
- OVERUSED STRENGTH
- OMIT PSYCHOLOGICAL SAFETY
- ONLY VALUE "YES" PEOPLE

S
- STOPPED LISTENING
- SELFISH VS SERVANT
- STOPPED DEVELOPING FUTURE LEADERS

E
- EGO OUT OF CONTROL
- EXERCISES BAD SAY/DO RATIO
- EXECUTIVE PRESENCE IS NO LONGER ROLE MODELING THE RIGHT BEHAVIORS

JOURNAL REFLECTIONS
HOW TO STOP FROM LOSING IT

S
- SELF-DETECT
- SELF-CORRECT

T
- TRANSPARENT
- HIDE THE BALL

O
- ON GOING EFFORT
- SPORADIC EFFORT

P
- PEOPLE & PASSION
- PROFITS & PROCESS

Self-Detect/Self-Correct

Ratio on the self-awareness to see if you can detect the impact of a sub-optimal behavior and then correct it before someone else tells you to.

Transparent/Hide the Ball

Ratio on being authentic and vulnerable with no hidden agenda.

Ongoing Effort/Sporadic Effort

Ratio on being dedicated and all-in to make a positive change versus putting in occasional effort.

People & Passion/Profits & Process

Ratio to reinforce that people and their passions should never be sacrificed for financials. People are your most important assets.

FORMAL PROCESSES

Too many organizations rely on what I call "incidental leadership training." They assume that the hands-on practice of having to manage a group or groups of people will unavoidably create experienced-based learnings for an emerging leader.

This is, of course, ridiculous.

Effective organizations make leadership training part of their formal processes, or they make these processes readily available to their people.

Courageous leaders, for their part, have the internal fortitude to ask others for help rather than remaining at less than 100% effectiveness. It takes communities, villages, and coaches to keep up with the speed of information.

The specific formal processes that have been found most effective are coaching and mentoring.

52%	Coaching and Mentoring
49%	Action Learning/Development
39%	Assessment & Feedback
34%	High-Potential Programs
24%	Exposure to Senior Executives[36]

THE BEST COMPANIES ARE BEST POSITIONED FOR TALENT

Here are the top four activities that the best companies encourage for leadership:

1. Leaders create a work climate that motivates their employees to do their best.
2. Their organizations actively manage a pool of successors for mission-critical roles.

3. People at all levels of the organization have an opportunity to develop and practice the capabilities needed to lead others.
4. A sufficient number of qualified candidates are ready to assume open leadership positions at all levels.

THE VALUE OF COACHING AND MENTORING IN DEVELOPING LEADERS

Whether you are coaching or mentoring, it takes a lot of courage for the person being coached to ask for help. Employees have reached out to me for guidance in countless leadership development sessions.

My mindset; always remember that they proactively came to me—recognizing that had to take a lot of guts—and to acknowledge that in the initial conversation. They were comfortable enough to share their issue with me and came to value the trust we had established; i.e., that their secret would be kept strictly confidential.

TWO EXAMPLES WORTH SHARING

1. An employee reached out to say he had been discriminated against and felt uncomfortable, undervalued, and unmotivated to come back to the job. Think about what *you* would do or say if someone said this to you. I listened, offered understanding, and then we brainstormed how to move forward in the best way. I then had to take action since discrimination to any employee has absolutely no place in the companies I work for. It did end up as a formal affirmative action complaint, and the issue was resolved with corrective action implemented. As I look back, I'm reminded once again how much courage it took to initiate this conversation.
2. Another employee reached out from a coaching session we had more than 10 years ago with this recollection:

> *"You called me into your office for one of our many impromptu coaching sessions (which I loved and miss), and you told me to slow down and take the time to self-reflect. As a recent college grad, who was new to corporate America and trying to make an impact, I did not know what that meant at the time, but fast-forward 10 years later, that coaching session now resonates. Thank You!"*

Just another example of how courage displayed long ago still provides a vivid memory.

OPTIMIZE THE "AFTER" LEARNING

One of the best practices in adult learning is what happens *after* learning. The subtle use of reminders plays a key role in retention—and it is part of the "repeat to remember and remember to repeat" mantra that makes the Four Loops of Learning so effective.[37]

Companies can achieve positive results when they develop and sustain positive habits that reinforce the new behaviors. In *The Power of Habit* by Charles Duhigg, a whole chapter, "Keystone Habits, or the Ballad of Paul O'Neill," explains how ingraining basic safety habits at Alcoa helped improve the bottom line—because the few "**keystone habits**" were easy to remember. These habits, regularly implemented and repeated, caused positive ripple results across the board.[38]

GET GOING NOW

Every day you delay implementing positive change is another day you can never regain. Is it somewhat scary to change, even if it's an improvement? Absolutely—and that's why we stress the COURAGE to lead.

> **"IF YOU QUANTIFY ONE THING FOR YOUR CUSTOMERS, QUANTIFY THE COST OF DELAY."**
>
> **- DON REINERTSEN**[39]

GET REALLY GOOD AT IMPLEMENTATION

> "IN REAL LIFE, STRATEGY IS ACTUALLY VERY STRAIGHTFORWARD. YOU PICK A GENERAL DIRECTION AND IMPLEMENT LIKE HELL."
>
> — JACK WELCH

G

GET REALLY GOOD AT IMPLEMENTATION

GET OUTSIDE YOUR COMFORT ZONE

The US Navy SEALs have a saying; "Get comfortable being uncomfortable."

During their training, SEALs do something called "surf torture," where everyone links arms and lays down in the cold ocean, remaining there until they reach the early stages of hypothermia. They often do this *daily* before taking on whatever tasks are scheduled.

> "COMFORT IS FREQUENTLY THE ENEMY OF GREATNESS. WHEN YOU CHOOSE TO DEFAULT TO COMFORT, YOU ARE CHOOSING TO BE LESS EFFECTIVE IN YOUR LIFE."
>
> - TODD HENRY[40]

No one's asking you to go to that sort of physical extreme, but here is a fact; stimulation and learning lives *outside* of your comfort zone. To grow, that's where you have to go regularly.

Most often, people are not afraid of the actual *consequences* they envision. They are actually *afraid of the feeling itself*. That bit of anxiety, when you are not in the comfortable pocket; that brief flash of apprehension, because you are attempting something new with no guarantee of success; the possibility of looking less than perfect.

Todd Henry has written some tremendous books about enriching your professional and personal lives that I highly recommend. In *Die Empty: Unleash Your Best Work Every Day*, Henry describes the work of Dr. Karl Pillemer, who interviewed hundreds of people, advanced in age, which he classified as "experts" due to their life experiences. He asked them to reflect on what they were most proud of and what they regretted most about past choices.

"The experts concur on this one point," Dr. Pillemer concluded. "*Say yes*. As far as work is concerned, those experts who were happiest about their career can point to a decision where they were tempted to say no, where staying the course was more comfortable and less risky, but they finally decided to give it a go."[41]

Unfortunately, we are biologically wired to seek the safest, least resistant path (remember the Rider). Nevertheless, very little learning can be acquired in our cozy little bubble.

CONVERT LEARNING INTO ACTION

> "WORDS MAY SHOW A MAN'S WIT, BUT ACTIONS, HIS MEANING."
> - BEN FRANKLIN

THE IMPORTANCE OF ACTION-BASED LEARNING

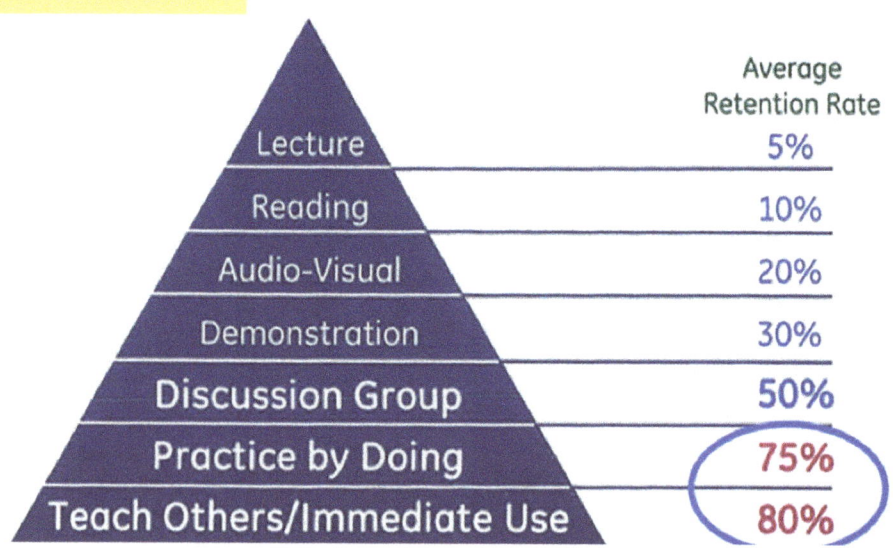

	Average Retention Rate
Lecture	5%
Reading	10%
Audio-Visual	20%
Demonstration	30%
Discussion Group	50%
Practice by Doing	75%
Teach Others/Immediate Use	80%

Source: Jeanne Meister, Corporate Universities [42]

As destructive as hiding in your comfort zone is, you also wreak havoc from the inability to *stop* doing things that are unproductive, because they're... comfortable. Here is where *unlearning* at the speed of change is vital.

But how best to learn and "unlearn?" It turns out that successful, courageous leaders actually schedule "out of the comfort zone" time into their work lives. They make a habit of failing quickly, failing often, and moving on to the next challenge, invigorated and enriched by the experience. They view the lessons of failure as a strategic asset.

> "THE MEDIOCRE TEACHER TELLS. THE GOOD TEACHER EXPLAINS. THE SUPERIOR TEACHER DEMONSTRATES. THE GREAT TEACHER INSPIRES."
> - WILLIAM ARTHUR WARD

They don't stop there, however. As seen in the diagram above, merely reading or attending a presentation is not enormously "sticky," in terms of converting learnings to behavior. Rather, action-based activities are the key to making things stick. It can be as simple as a discussion, and as elemental as actually "doing" the behavior desired.

The best technique, other than the immediate use of a specific learning, is taking the time to *teach others the same skill*.

LEVERAGE THE POWER OF SPACING

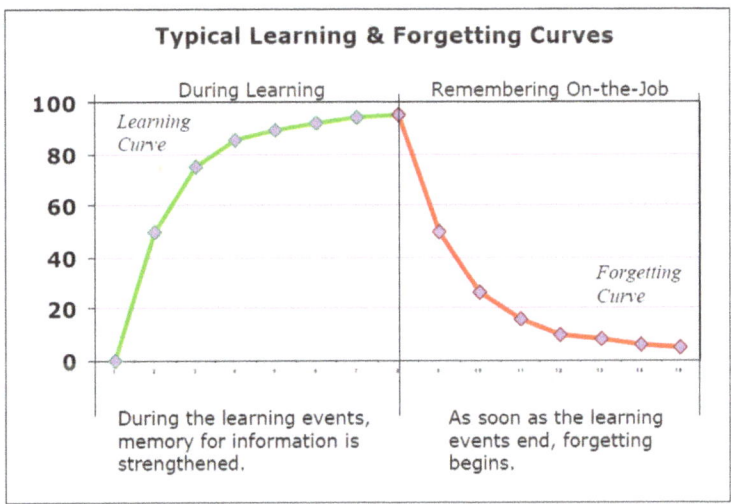

(also known as the Ebbinghaus forgetting curve)

I bet you didn't need a graph to agree with this Harvard study. During learning events, the information memory line goes up and up; after learning events, forgetting begins in earnest.

Now, let's look at a revised graph:

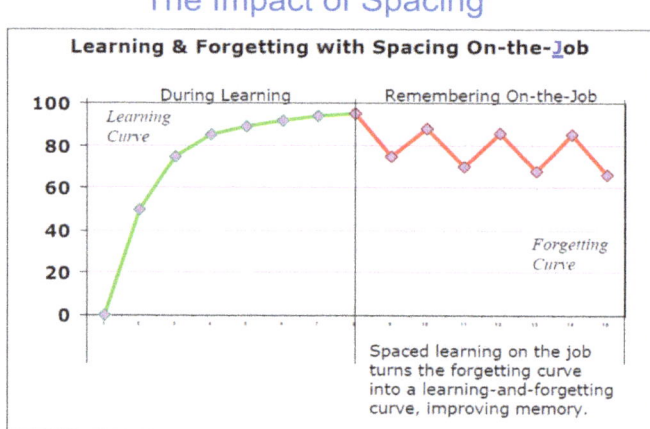

Now the line stays elevated. How? Simply by adding intervals of review or repetition at six subsequent points after learning.

Professor Cecil Alec Mace published *The Psychology of Study* (1969) that was first to put forward the notion that spaced repetition could be used for improving learning.

"Perhaps the most important discoveries are those which relate to the appropriate distribution of the periods of study ... Acts of revision should be spaced in gradually increasing intervals, roughly intervals of one day, two days, four days, eight days, and so on."[43]

Over time, this has been systematized to six points of review in Professor Mace's study, and, as demonstrated in the retention rate study, your best bet is to do so via discussion, actual practice, and teaching others—all activities that encourage team building and collaboration, it turns out.

Get Really Good at Implementation

The courageous leader recognizes the value of stepping out of his or her comfort zone to enable lifelong learning and "unlearning" and builds these practices into his or her routines.

10

ENCOURAGE ITERATION, NOT PERFECTION

> "MAKE THE MOST OF THE BEST AND LEAST OF THE WORST."
>
> ROBERT LOUIS STEVENSON

Four Loop Learning: Courage to Lead

ENCOURAGE ITERATION, NOT PERFECTION

NEW TRIAL & ERROR HEADSET

Here are four examples of reframing how you look at things:

PURSUIT FOR PERFECTION
↓
LEARN QUICKLY FROM ITERATION

FEAR OF FAILURE
↓
TREAT FAILURES LIKE STRATEGIC ASSETS

TECHNOLOGY/ENGINEERING LED
↓
CUSTOMER DRIVEN INPUT

FAILURE = END OF CAREER
↓
FAILURE = KEY TO LONGEVITY

One of the key changes you will see when you begin to regularly leave your comfort zone is a set of new approaches to how you confront problems and even failures.

Take, for example, the pursuit of perfection that has tripped up so many otherwise capable leaders.

> "NO BATTLE PLAN EVER SURVIVES CONTACT WITH THE ENEMY."
> - FIELD MARSHAL HELMUTH KARL BERNHARD GRAF VON MOLTKE

If you haven't learned this by now, I'll let you in on two little secrets:

1. There is no perfect.
2. Many times the extra energy expended on the pursuit of perfection is time lost when good is good enough.

For many, this is a very hard pill to swallow. Taking your emphasis off the pursuit of instant perfection, however, and instead placing it squarely on SOLID, STEADY ITERATION means you attain goal after goal on the way to better results.

Professor Amy Edmondson of Harvard University studied how 16 hospitals implemented a new, non-invasive open-heart surgery technique called "minimally invasive cardiac surgery" (MICS). Basically, this revolutionary new approach allows the heart to be repaired without having to open up the patient's chest. MICS patients are released from the hospital after four days instead of eight and reach full recovery in three weeks rather than two months. The technique requires that the entire surgical team completely rethink their approach to heart surgery; a catheter with a deflated balloon is threaded through the groin, and the surgeon approaches the heart through a small, three-inch incision between the ribs. For much of the procedure, the surgeon is "flying blind" and must rely heavily upon the anesthesiologist to monitor, for example, the progress of the balloon toward the heart.

Edmondson found that, while some hospitals learned and embraced the new technique, several failed and retreated to the old method. The key to success, she found, was the fact that the successful teams adopted what Edmondson called a "learning frame." Members of these teams approached MICS as something that would be very difficult at first but would get less daunting over time if they were open to changing how they did nearly every aspect of their jobs.

Encourage Iteration, Not Perfection

Doctor "A" wore a camera on his head so the team could review procedures easily afterward. He also scheduled the first six MICS cases in a single week so there would be rapid repetition of learnings and skills and kept a core team together with new persons rotating in only one at a time. The result was he and his hospital had—and have—tremendous ongoing success with MICS.

Doctor "B" admitted to being interested in MICS for outward-focused, competitive reasons. "It's a marketing thing. People want to know we can do it." Team members talked about "keeping up with the Joneses." Dr. B. implemented the MICS procedure while *still* splitting the patient's breastbone—the single most invasive and damaging aspect of the old technique. One of the nurses remarked, "Doctor 'B' is a creature of habit." These old, comfortable habits eventually won out, and MICS was abandoned at the Doctor 'B' hospital.

Edmondson's findings were clear. The teams that felt they had to "get it right the first time" and derived their motivation from the chance to "perform, to shine, or to execute perfectly" were the teams that failed.

On the other hand, successful teams focused on learning and didn't assume they'd master the complicated procedure quickly. They a) anticipated challenges, stumbles, and discomfort; b) embraced iteration, knowing that mastery would be a process; and c) treated procedural missteps—"failures"—as useful assets.

Edmondson's *learning frame* (see above) proved to be the key.[44]

It requires what I call a "trial-and-error headset," as seen in the previous graphic above.

In our heart-surgery example, you'll find the "keeping up with the Joneses" correlation in "Technology/engineering led" vs. "Customer input driven;" Doctor "B" and his team were led more by the *idea and appearance* of being cutting-edge than they were by the results possible for their patients!

Failure is not the end. Make failure your friend in your processes, and you and your team will succeed again and again.

PASSING THE "COURAGE TO LEAD" TORCH

In the song "Anthem," poet Leonard Cohen exclaims, "Forget your perfect offering. There is a crack, a crack in everything. That's how the light gets in."

Likewise, in *Star Wars: Episode VIII–The Last Jedi* (2017), Yoda counsels Luke Skywalker to "pass on what you have learned. Strength. Mastery. But weakness, folly, failure as well. Yes, failure most of all. The greatest teacher, failure is. Luke, we are what they grow beyond. That is the true burden of all masters." [45]

My generation, the boomers, certainly have given the next generations—Gen X (1965-1979), xennials (1975-1985), millennials (1980-1994), Gen Z (1995-2012), and Gen Alpha (2013-2025)—plenty of failure to grow beyond.

Even so, these words from President John F. Kennedy still ring true nearly 60 years after he said them on January 20, 1961.

"Let the word go forth from this time and place, to friend and foe alike, that the torch has been passed to a new generation of Americans… we shall pay any price, bear any burden, meet any hardship, support any friend, oppose any foe to assure the survival and the success of liberty."

Life isn't a sprint—and it isn't even a marathon, contrary to what you may have heard. Really, it's more like an Olympic relay race. Each generation brings its unique strengths and strategies to its leg within the framework of the overall effort. The handoffs matter; they can make or break a team's success.

Right now, millennials are running the "anchor leg"—one in which they will need to come from behind to get back ahead while still remembering to pace themselves carefully. So let's digress just a bit to see how.

MILLENNIAL GENERATION =

TIP of the Spear / TIP the Balance:

Transformation	**(Tech as a way of Life)**
Inspiration	**(Iteration as a Vocation)**
Pollination (B the B!)	**(Pathways to Promotion)**

ITERATION, NOT PERFECTION: AN ESSENTIALLY MILLENNIAL RAISON D'ÊTRE

Every generation looks at the following generation through a somewhat cynical, world-weary lens.[46]

Imagine the Greatest Generation, who fought World War II, observing the angst of the baby boomers. Next, the boomers derided Generation "X" (born in the mid-'60s) as being lazy, directionless posers. Generation "Y" followed (born in the mid-'70s), seemingly less moody, but accused of a "sense of entitlement." And Generation "X" and "Y," for their part, blame baby boomers for pulverizing the traditional American Dream.

And now, millennials. According to researchers Neil Howe and William Strauss, a millennial is anyone born between 1982 and 2004. In 2015, they've officially overtaken baby boomers as the nation's largest living generation.[47]

I can almost hear the judgments; after all, why should their generation be spared the disparagement every previous cohort has weathered from their predecessors?

Go ahead; get it out of your system. "Self-absorbed." "Entitled." "Impatient." "Lazy." "Over-educated and under-employed."

Now that we got that out of the way, I can tell you that you are wrong.

Here are some *actual* millennial characteristics you should know:

- Single
- Living with others or at home
- Only interested in urban living but challenged with the impact of COVID-19 and the increase in suburban living
- 65% vote Democratic
- Believe work and play are interchangeable parts of life
- Want to be promoted every 9-12 months
- Don't expect perfection but rather iteration *(see above)*
- Value experiences over expertise
- Accomplish things in groups
- Are visual

Here are a few examples of how millennials view baby boomers:

- Less formally educated (due to differences in employment and financial well-being, according to a Pew study)
- Conservative regarding social and racial issues, including Black Lives Matter, equality for women, immigrants, LGBT+, and disabled people, as well as environmental issues
- Value financial gain and individual wealth versus community or climate-change issues, perhaps tied to a fear of change or personal loss economically
- Their emphasis on progress and performance is debilitating to younger generations in the workforce

TECHNOLOGY IS A WAY OF LIFE

The millennial generation is fearless and willing to try new things. They are so used to the fast-paced nature of their smartphone devices and constant updates of information that they quickly adjust to rapid change.

Contrast this with the boomer generation (1947-1964) that is more fixated on process and procedure and possesses a risk-averse mindset, whereas millennials like to experiment with new things. Millennials learn quickly from their attempts and use the experience and knowledge as a stair-step into something else.

An expression I've used:

"For boomers, when they fail, they think their career is at an end; for millennials, when they fail, the learnings are their friend."

Millennials grew up in an economic recession, raised by the competitive and hard-working boomers. The ability to adapt to fast-paced change, especially technological change, is a leg up in a racing world where education and experience are expected from millennials. This mindset is crucial for surviving a pandemic in one's early or mid-career, not to mention the undiscussed issues of climate change, race, and social justice, as well as financial hardship.

Let's talk about what the typical millennial is facing in terms of debt. The average amount of school debt jumped from $12,000 for the class of 1993 to nearly $27,000 for the class of 2012.[48]

This reality differs from the one faced by boomers and creates a mindset that focuses on quick and steady advancement to stay ahead of the bills.

So be aware that rejection of "slow and steady" isn't primarily a philosophical stance; it doesn't work from a mathematical viewpoint either. Millennials are looking for organizations and careers that offer an efficient path to getting "into the black" while still offering challenges and opportunities to explore a wide range of experiences.

One other perspective I want to share are some journal notes I took from Tim Denning[49] on the future of leadership from a millennial's perspective. In addition to being data-driven, technology-led, and involved in a challenging global economy, they still feel strongly about their preferences of leadership.

1. Leadership is about inspiration, not domination.
2. Leadership is about transformation, not manipulation.

EXAMPLE OF COURAGE BY A MILLENNIAL LEADER

Christina Mealey is the Clinical Manager, BSN, RN, on the 11th Floor Adult Inpatient Unit at Massachusetts Eye & Ear who has cared for me multiple times during my medical journey. Her leadership, and the environment she fosters, ensured her nurses made decisions that played a big role in my healing and recovery.

Christina shared as a young leader in healthcare that several times she had had to dig deep within herself to find the courage to make decisions. In her experience, individuals sometimes have to make difficult choices for the greater good. Making decisions that are unpopular yet necessary is tough; however, dealing with the human responses of these decisions is difficult in its own way.

Encourage Iteration, Not Perfection

According to Christina, having the courage to do the right thing, even if it means having difficult conversations, is hard, especially while trying to maintain a positive relationship with staff. I have come to find out, however, that in doing this, it has ultimately grown my relationship with staff, as it has created a sense of trust and respect among the team. People respond well to structure, consistency, and fairness; especially in times of crisis. They will look to leadership for guidance—and leadership needs to have to courage to guide people gracefully.

In her experience, leadership roles in nursing are complex, as you must find a balance between the nurse that you are, and the leader you are becoming. Coming to peace with the merging of these two roles is something that takes trial and error. Learning to lead by example, to never ask your staff to do something you have not done yourself, supporting the staff to provide the highest level of care to our patients, and identifying and then acting on issues that do not result in high quality care, are all critical in forming a strong nursing team.

She has also found out that, while leading takes courage, it takes courage to know when to delegate and let your staff run point. Sometimes the best leadership is knowing when *not* to lead, and to encourage your staff to grow. For me, working hard to create an overall environment where people want to work, has been one of my top priorities.

When people enjoy their work environment, they are more connected and dedicated to helping build that positive workspace. When leadership and staff are in harmony, communicating effectively, the teamwork is felt, most importantly, by the patients whom we serve.

BE THE BEE

Sir Francis Bacon was speaking of approaches to science when he used the analogy of the ant, spider, and bee, but we could easily apply these three insects to the world of leadership and learning.

Four Loop Learning: Courage to Lead

Are you an ANT, SPIDER, or BEE in your organization?

If you are an ant, you gather material and use it. Pick it up where you find it, bring it back to the anthill, and then start over again—an ant does not evaluate beyond judging whether whatever is being gathered can fit into the anthill, and concentrates its effort on taking that which others have made. When a leader relies almost exclusively on the ideas of others, and brings back only what he or she thinks will "fit," he or she is an ant.

> "THOSE WHO HAVE HANDLED SCIENCES HAVE BEEN EITHER MEN OF EXPERIMENT OR MEN OF DOGMAS. THE MEN OF EXPERIMENT ARE LIKE THE ANT, THEY ONLY COLLECT AND USE; THE REASONERS RESEMBLE SPIDERS, WHO MAKE COBWEBS OUT OF THEIR OWN SUBSTANCE. BUT THE BEE TAKES A MIDDLE COURSE: IT GATHERS ITS MATERIAL FROM THE FLOWERS OF THE GARDEN AND OF THE FIELD BUT TRANSFORMS AND DIGESTS IT BY A POWER OF ITS OWN."
>
> – SIR FRANCIS BACON [50]

As a spider, you build complicated constructs out of nothing but yourself—literally *traps*. Abandoned cobwebs tell the story; spiders have no long-term allegiance to their creation after it has ensnared prey that can fray the web. The leader whose thinking is confined to his or her own opinions is a spider.

The bee, however, travels far and wide to select specific pollen that, by itself, may not appear intrinsically valuable. Careful choices are made, the correct pollen is retrieved from the correct flower, and the bee returns to a purposeful hive that is prepared to accept and convert the raw material to liquid gold. Furthermore, all of the bee's encounters enrich the flowers that provide raw materials.

The courageous leader is transformative and purposeful, positively affecting both sides of the transaction. **Be the Bee!**

11 EXAMPLE OF COURAGE IN HEALTHCARE

During the process of writing this book, I had many valuable people in my network provide their experiences and point of view on courage. I want to share the following with you, which really provided excellent context on courage in the medical field by an exceptional doctor who saved my life.

Dr. Tessa Hadlock is Professor, Department Head of Ontology and Laryngology, and Director of Facial Plastic and Reconstructive Surgery at Harvard Medical School.

Five Facets of Courage
- Written by Dr. Tessa Hadlock

While so many leadership traits are elusive, nuanced, and difficult to name, one theme common among effective leaders is courage. As an emerging surgical leader, I have come to appreciate different facets of courage partway through the course of an academic career. Five basic features of courage have taken shape over the

> "COURAGE: THE MOST IMPORTANT OF ALL THE VIRTUES, BECAUSE WITHOUT COURAGE, YOU CAN'T PRACTICE ANY OTHER VIRTUE CONSISTENTLY."
>
> — MAYA ANGELOU

course of my journey to date, sometimes in sequence, sometimes in parallel, with some phases that still lay ahead. A brief word on each feature may be relevant to readers interested in courage.

1. **A leader has the courage to express a vision.** It is a gift to imagine and articulate a better or more effective way of doing things, but can also be risky or frightening. Surgery is a storied field, steeped in deep tradition based on experience, wisdom, observation, literature, and careful thought. Proposing shifts, large or small, in technique, protocol, or paradigm, to surgeons, takes tremendous courage; surgery attracts people who are pretty sure they are right most or all of the time and are among the healthcare providers most resistant to change. Additionally, surgery has long held a hierarchical or militaristic structure, where top-down management of teams has been the model. Emerging leaders may face resistance if their expression of new ideas and vision is not timed with their "rank" at the time of its introduction. Silence or submission, however, will result in lost opportunities for growth, improvement, and innovation in surgery; some of the best innovations have come from surgeons with the courage to express a new vision.

2. **A leader possesses courage to express a dissenting view** when that view is appropriate to the bigger picture. It can be difficult in a group of strong personalities and vocal personas to find courage to express a view counter to the one held by the majority or by the powerful and influential members of a group. When surgeons come together in discussion, they tend to focus on issues relevant to particular practices, small groups, and micro-environments. In surgical leadership, considering the needs of the individual practices in the context of the larger practice, hospital, or health system is critically important. Often, a leader can appreciate what is best for the entire system, even when it is counter to the local objectives of the smaller surgical group. He or she must possess not only courage to express

this dissenting, broader view with grace and sensitivity, but also the wisdom to articulate the broader-range benefits in ways that permit others to ultimately appreciate the rationale for the alternate view or strategy. Courage to express a dissenting view must be closely coupled with eloquent and genuine communication skills.

3. **A leader has courage to accept the limitations and different maturity levels of their constituents** and provide them the time and space to grow effectively. This patience with others may not be a natural attribute to surgical leaders, since they tend to be can-do, get-it-done-yesterday type people. Patience to tolerate some nastiness, rage, intolerance, and immaturity is pivotally important to helping a group of surgeons mature individually and as a group. In the words of Ruth Bader Ginsburg, it is good to be "a little deaf" when people bringing more emotion than is called for say things more emphatically or from a more entrenched perspective than they will ultimately take. Learning to control reacting to such situations and to avoid responding with similar overly charged emotional language is likely the hardest leadership lesson I have had to learn. As leaders, we cannot change our constituents. They can certainly change themselves, growing and maturing with good modeling and motivation, but a leader's responsibility is to create an environment permissive to this growth. Rushing someone else's growth is like trying to potty-train a newborn or teach a toddler to drive a car; the endeavor will simply not be successful. It takes deep courage to believe in the growth potential of the group and to do everything possible to cultivate group development.

4. **A leader has the courage to look inward.** Surgeons spend their careers achieving; curing disease, becoming masters of a craft, orchestrating an operating room, refining techniques, and running things. Historically, the ability to look

inward, to become more self-aware, was neither selected for nor rewarded. The louder one spoke, the surer one was, the better. As surgery has developed in its humanity toward its trainees, and as surgical departments have had to interact on more sophisticated and less dogmatic terms with other departments in hospital systems, the militant model has simply disintegrated. We, as a group, have had to learn to listen, to contextualize, to relax, to step back. Most importantly, we have had to learn to look inward, the same way others need to, for the insights that make us better surgeons, leaders, partners, and role models. Of course, some surgeons have maintained good awareness of the evolving times, the shifting work climate toward more inclusive atmospheres, and the increased need for sensitivity in articulating workplace expectations. Others, like me, lacked the situational awareness to recognize the massive transformation of workplace standards and expectations over a few years, and were forced to abandon old habits and intolerances more abruptly. Either way, the field of surgery, and the place of surgical departments in the context of larger healthcare systems, has changed substantively for the better, and surgeons are well-coached on looking inward, at hearing how their voices might sound to colleagues and subordinates, and modulating them to positive effect. Of all the gifts of a career in academic surgery, the most fruitful gift has been coaching in the ability to look inward, and through increased self-awareness, become a more effective leader. Looking inward takes tremendous courage, but must be embraced as a longitudinal endeavor.

5. **A leader has the courage to step down**, to let leadership come to an end, to permit a changing of the guard, to relinquish power and influence, to step back. Surgeons, as a group, have not routinely found this courage. Leadership training programs emphasize that no good strategy exists for helping surgeons find their end game. End game may refer to the end of a leadership role for those who discover

they are either not good at it, not interested in it, or both—or it may refer to the end of an active surgical clinical career. Either way, reverence, complacency, or lack of courage among other leaders to create a change can lead to surgeons lingering in inappropriate administrative or clinical roles. As yet, I have no special insight into finding this courage, perhaps because it takes an entire career to develop this insight—or simply because I have not yet had to face this particular dilemma. Nevertheless, a discussion about courage in surgical leadership necessarily must contain this final courage.

12

THE POWER OF REFLECTION

Why Handwrite?

I often get asked why I handwrite the journals—especially when we are in the hyper-connected world of the digital age—and the reason is quite simple. You simply retain more learning when you physically handwrite versus type on a keyboard.[53]

I also feel like technology has taken over my life, and journaling is my own personal rebellion against a life ruled by digital hyper-connectivity with 24x7 availability. Don't get me wrong, I also live on my iPhone, iPad and Mac, but it is also quite enjoyable to stay connected and learn with a nostalgic practice of the past—writing with pen on paper.

> "A PERSONAL JOURNAL IS AN IDEAL ENVIRONMENT IN WHICH TO BECOME. IT IS A PERFECT PLACE FOR YOU TO THINK, FEEL, DISCOVER, EXPAND, REMEMBER AND DREAM."
>
> - BRAD WILCOX[52]

FOUR LOOP LEARNING

One of the principles of effective adult learning that I learned is "to repeat to remember and remember to repeat."[55] The journals provide me with multiple loops of learning in which the myriad reference points help me remember more of

> "WRITING IN A JOURNAL EACH DAY ALLOWS YOU TO DIRECT YOUR FOCUS TO WHAT YOU ACCOMPLISHED, WHAT YOU ARE GRATEFUL FOR AND WHAT YOU'RE COMMITTED TO DOING BETTER TOMORROW. THUS, YOU WILL DEEPLY ENJOY YOUR JOURNEY EACH DAY."
>
> — HAL ELROD [51]

> "JOURNAL WRITING, WHEN IT BECOMES A RITUAL FOR TRANSFORMATION, IS NOT ONLY LIFE-CHANGING BUT LIFE-EXPANDING."
>
> - JEN WILLIAMSON[54]

the important linkages and connections than if I left it to chance.

The journals represent the following four loops of learning, which took 20 years to create, refine, and shape a framework that I could count on and truly enjoy.

Loop 1–RECORD: the art of actually handwriting in the journals and recording things that are relevant in your life, whether personal or professional. This is also sometimes referred to as note-taking.

Loop 2–REFLECT: summarizing the most important learnings from every 50 pages (referred to as Stop & Reflects in my customized journals), where I also cross-reference to multiple H's (i.e., head, heart, hand, health, humility, high-performance teams). This stage can also be referred to as note-making, as I draw conclusions from the content to understand things at a higher level. This is where I do a lot of divergent and convergent thinking with the recorded content.

Loop 3–ACT: summarizing the most significant learning in each journal from the collection of the most important Stop & Reflects every 50 pages. Each journal averages 250 pages with four Stop & Reflects. Each Stop & Reflect has approximately 10 learnings, so that provides you with 40 key learnings. The goal is to get down to the *one most important learning* to put into action to become a higher impact leader. This narrowing down keeps getting harder and harder as the content gets richer and richer.

Loop 4–SHARE: when I use the learnings to share and teach with others. This fourth loop is my favorite because it is so rewarding to help others–in fact, the core component in my personal mantra to be a servant leader.

If this basic introduction to my Four Loop Learning model interests you as an engaging way to begin and learn how to journal successfully, consider putting this book's advice to use through the Leadership Reflections Kit, composed of a customized journal and instruction manual called Reflection Points, that can be found at www.FourLoopLearning.com.

My good friend and author of *Stretch: How to Future-Proof Yourself for Tomorrow's Workplace*, Dr. Karie Willyerd, highlighted my multiple loop process in her book as a way to use multiple-loop learning to impact the stickiness of your learning. [56]

THE ADVANTAGES OF LOOKING FOR X AND FINDING Y

One of the most enjoyable aspects of the journal is coming across something of value when I am looking for something else. Countless times, when I'm looking for one thing and find something else, that's even better. The rediscovered page really takes my current search and thinking to a much higher dimension. Connecting the dots is one of my favorite activities with the journals, which enables me to curate favorite quotes, relevant articles, and up-and-coming leadership teachings into a unique and digestible perspective for my mentees. This is exactly what I did when I started to converge my journal content on the attributes of Courage as a leadership advantage.

> "JOURNALING CAN BE AN EXCELLENT WAY TO INCREASE SELF-AWARENESS, DISCOVER AND CHANGE HABITS."
> - AKIROQ BROST

13 COMMONLY ASKED QUESTIONS

Throughout all my leadership development sessions over the past decade, I recorded the repeatedly asked questions. All connect to courageous leadership, so I want to provide you with these questions as well as my responses from multiple journal observations.

WHAT'S YOUR DEFINITION OF A GREAT LEADER?

So many terrific definitions exist for leadership! I created a version based on leveraging the content from other thought leaders I've recorded in my journals throughout the years, such as:

> "Leadership, at its core, is about making other people better as a result of your presence—and making sure that the impact lasts in your presence."
>
> ~ Frances Frei of Harvard

> "The foundation of effective leadership is thinking through the organization's mission, defining it, and establishing it clearly and visibly. The leader then sets goals, sets priorities, and maintains the standards."
>
> ~ Peter Drucker

"WITHOUT COURAGE, WISDOM BEARS NO FRUIT."

BALTASAR GRACIAN

> "The role of leaders is not to get others to follow them, but to empower them to lead."
>
> ~ Bill George (ex-CEO of Medtronic's)

> "Average leaders raise the bar on themselves, good leaders raise the bar for others, great leaders INSPIRE others to raise their own bar."
>
> ~ Orrin Woodward

> "A good leader is a person who takes a little more than share of the blame and a little less than share of the credit."
>
> ~ John Maxwell

> "A leader is someone who creates breakthroughs. Otherwise you are a manager."
>
> ~ Tony Robbins

> "Leadership is when you use talent, skills, and emotional intelligence to mobilize people to a common purpose."
>
> ~ Doris Kearns Goodwin

> "Leadership is the capacity to influence others to achieve a desired, often shared goal. Period."
>
> ~ Dr. Rick Lash

> "The task of leadership is not to put greatness into people, but to elicit it, for the greatness is there already."
>
> ~ John Buchan

So based upon these great contributions, my amalgamated definition of leadership is as follows and is expanded upon by the following quote from Mark Twain.

> "The two most important days in your life are the day you are born and the day you know why." ~Mark Twain

> "Leadership is enthusiastically connecting the goals of a company (or institution/school/team/etc.) to the people

who are dedicated to the work behind the cause. Great leaders inspire their employees, help them find their 'why' and constantly link purpose to their roles. When this happens, great outcomes can be invented, implemented, and sustained." ~Bob Cancalosi

I use empowering quotes from leaders across the globe to emphasize the values and relevance of ideas for new and beginning leaders, to help find a spark of inspiration for them.

WHO ARE YOUR LEADERSHIP ROLE MODELS?

My role models are a combination of the past and the present.

MY LEADERSHIP ROLE MODELS FROM THE PAST ARE:

> "WHEN YOU SEE SOMETHING THAT IS NOT RIGHT, NOT FAIR, NOT JUST, YOU HAVE TO SPEAK UP. YOU HAVE TO SAY SOMETHING, YOU HAVE TO DO SOMETHING."
> - JOHN LEWIS

Abraham Lincoln, for embracing his enemies.

Martin Luther King, for taking a stand and his lifetime commitment for social justice.

John Lewis, for his lifelong championship of human rights and having the courage to use 'Good Trouble' to oppose systemic racism.

John F. Kennedy, for creating a dream to land a man on the moon and return them home safely.

Peter Drucker, for numerous lessons on the difference between leadership and management.

> "SAVOR THE TASTE OF YOUR TRIUMPHS TODAY. DON'T JUST SWALLOW THE MOMENT WHOLE WITHOUT DIGESTING WHAT IS ACTUALLY HAPPENING HERE. LOOK DOWN OVER WHAT YOU CONQUERED AND APPRECIATE WHAT GOD HAS BROUGHT YOU THROUGH."
>
> **- CHADWICK BOSEMAN**

John McCain, for his dedication to service and his impactful quote on Americans; "There is more that unites us then divides us."

Chadwick Boseman, for continuing his passion of acting while pursuing cancer treatments.

Mother Teresa, for forgiveness, as we are not perfect.

My father, for showing me that great things can be accomplished in life with passion, commitment and a dedicated work ethic.

MY PRESENT-DAY LEADERSHIP ROLE MODELS ARE:

Warren Buffett, for his deliberate reflection time.

Jamie Dimon, for chairing the Business Council creation on the new "Purpose of an Organization".

Yvon Chouinard of Patagonia, for his commitment to sustainability.

The firefighters who rushed into buildings to save lives on 911.

The doctors, nurses and first responders who unselfishly gave their best efforts to save so many COVID-19 patients are also significant role models.

ALESSANDRA'S ROLE MODELS ARE:

Bob Cancalosi, my father, for challenging me to follow my dreams and write this book, and Barbara Cancalosi, my mother, for supporting the both of us on this journey and teaching me how to be courageous in times of adversity.

Alicia Garza and Opal Tometi, co-founders of Black Lives Matter, and every voice fighting for equality–you are heard.

José Andrés, a world-renowned chef dedicated to feeding those in need.

Alie Ward, for creating enthusiasm across every scientific field through her podcasts.

Women with power across the world–thank you to Greta Thunberg, Alexandria Ocasio-Cortez, Jacinda Ardern, Ayana Elizabeth Johnson and so many more.

CAN LEADERSHIP BE LEARNED?

Absolutely! It takes willingness to listen, learn, and reflect that your style can situationally align to the mission at hand. I learned from Professor Hitendra Wadhwa of Columbia University that really successful leaders all commit to regular practice with feedback and adjustments to changing conditions. An openness to learn, and adjusting your style and approach, can help leaders lead better!

WHAT ARE THE MAIN CHARACTERISTICS THAT DERAIL LEADERS?

I reference six derailers in the "A" of courage–always looking to improve. Most of the derailers are soft-skill issues (e.g., how you get along with people), and not the hard issues (e.g., strategy, investment, acquisitions) that you would typically view as the culprits.

WHAT ARE THE NEW LEADERSHIP SKILLS TO MASTER BY THE YEAR 2030?

First of all, I believe a core of leadership attributes will be timeless and always relevant, such as the ability to inspire others, have crucial conversations and develop the next wave of talent. The new skills in the future will be based upon being able to see what is needed at a particular time. Countless new jobs 10 years from now do not exist today, so we'll need leaders who can determine these skills ahead of time and start to build competency within their organizations *before* it is required.

IF YOU COULD SUMMARIZE THE ONE "MAGIC BULLET" OF GREAT LEADERSHIP EFFECTIVENESS, WHAT IS IT?

In my experience, there is not one silver bullet, yet I believe some essential components are required. First of all, the need to INSPIRE others to believe in themselves, to constantly stretch themselves, and to help them become the best they can be. And then ask if they HAVE IT?

Commonly Asked Questions

And if you do not HAVE IT, WHEN *will* you?

I found a common thread in my responses as well. Almost every approach, technique, mindset, guideline, etc. that I described contained an element of **boldness**. It became clear that successful leadership meant confronting fears and overcoming them—getting out of their respective comfort zones—on the way to best solutions and greater innovations. *People want to know how to accomplish this.*

> "THE BEST LIGHTNING ROD FOR YOUR PROTECTION IS YOUR OWN SPINE."
> - RALPH WALDO EMERSON

DO LEADERSHIP SKILLS COME NATURALLY TO SOME?

Research by John H. Zenger and his co-authors calculated that ~32% of leadership ability is genetically based, and the other 68% is based upon other factors, such as leadership development. [57]

When I'm asked the same question, my response is "undoubtedly." Clearly, the bulk of us, however, will benefit from guided focus into the principles and practices that build and reinforce great leaders over time. That's what the seven components of the *Courage to Lead* are all about.

HOW DOES ONE LEAD CHANGE WHEN PEOPLE ARE SO FIXED IN THEIR WAYS?

Show how the change is a good thing for the people who do not want to change. A burning platform is a great start that has to be kindled, endowed with deep purpose, and then shared with the employees who have to live with the changes. Asking for their input is critical to get their "skin in the game" if you really want a sustainable outcome. You can achieve great momentum if you can find a few Influencers in the organization to sponsor and advocate the change.

HOW CAN WE FIND THE TIME TO ACCELERATE OUR LEARNING PRACTICES WHEN WE FEEL SATURATED?

Take a very realistic inventory of where you spend your time. Accelerating your learning (i.e., learning and unlearning faster than change) is critical to success. Stop doing things that do not directly support the learnings and do more things that do—it's really that easy. Where do you spend your time? Do more highly leveraged activities, where accomplishing one thing can help build momentum in many other areas.

WHAT SHOULD I READ, AND WHAT WEBSITES SHOULD I FREQUENT TO KEEP MYSELF CURRENT AND RELEVANT?

I recommend the 5-4-3-2-1 process:

> **5-4-3-2-1 ANALYSIS**
> TO STAY **RELEVANT**
> 5 DIFFERENT NEWS SOURCES
> 4 CONVERSATIONS WITH SMART PEOPLE
> 3 BOOKS READ PER YEAR
> 2 DEDICATED WEEKS OF TRAINING
> 1 REFLECTIVE JOURNAL TO RECORD YOUR KEY LEARNINGS

Commonly Asked Questions

I actually have another version of 5-4-3-2-1 embedded into the custom journal I created. In this model, the breakdown is as follows:

5 The five most important people to add to my network

4 The four things I learn at any major event

3 The three things that can help my mentees go a little bit deeper in fulfilling their ambitions.

2 The two things I did well and the two things I can do better

1 The one and *only* one thing I will commit to doing better in the future.

Here is what the pages look like in the Leadership reflections journal. The journal contains three separate sets to capture the learnings from multiple educational sessions. [58]

EVENT: _____   DATE: _____

5-4-3-2-1

5 THE FIVE MOST POWERFUL PROFESSIONALS TO ADD TO YOUR NETWORK:
1. _____
2. _____
3. _____
4. _____
5. _____

4 THE FOUR MOST IMPORTANT THINGS YOU LEARNED FROM THIS SESSION:
1. _____
2. _____
3. _____
4. _____

Four Loop Learning: Courage to Lead

```
EVENT:_____          DATE:_____

        5-4-3-2-1

THE THREE MOST IMPORTANT THINGS YOU      3
LEARNED TO ACCELERATE YOUR AMBITION AND
THE AMBITION OF OTHERS:
1._____
2._____
3._____


THE TWO THINGS YOU DID WELL AS A LEADER, 2
AND TWO THINGS YOU CAN DO BETTER:
1._____
2._____                    (DID WELL)

1._____
2._____                    (DO BETTER)


IF YOU LOOK BACK TEN YEARS FROM NOW,     1
WHAT IS THE ONE THING YOU WILL REMEMBER:
1._____
```

HOW DO WE BUILD A COMPELLING PURPOSE STATEMENT THAT ENERGIZES THE TEACHERS AND THE STUDENTS?

Look at a few different purpose statements and see what words inspire you; then use the most inspirational words to create a draft. Vet your draft with inputs from five trusted friends and then co-create the final product with the leadership team. The next step is to have the courage to launch.

HOW DO I DEAL WITH FAILURE?

Failure is a very important ingredient of success. The two types of failure are 1) when the learnings from failure are not shared with others, to prevent them from making the same mistake; and 2) not trying again. I always try to remember the quote from Thomas Edison on inventing the right filament for the light bulb.

"I have not failed 10,000 times. I have not failed once. I have succeeded in proving that those 10,000 ways will not work. When I have eliminated the ways that will not work, I will find the way that will work."

Here are a few more of my favorite collected journal quotes:

FAIL = First Attempt In Learning

Failure is the opportunity to begin again more intelligently.
~ Henry Ford

The fear of failure is more destructive than fear itself.
~ Anonymous

FEAR = False Education Appearing Real

If you fail to plan, you plan to fail.
~ Benjamin Franklin

Failure is not the opposite of success, it's part of it.
~QEZ

Mistakes are a fact of life. It's the response to error that counts.
~Nikki Giovanni

Men succeed when they realize that their failures are the preparation for their victories.
~ Ralph Waldo Emerson

Only those who risk going too far can possibly find out how far one can go.
~ T. S. Eliot

It is impossible to live without failing at something, unless you live so cautiously that you might as well not have lived at all—in which case you fail by default.
~ JK Rowling

To live a creative life, we must lose our fear of being wrong.
~Joseph Chilton Pearce

It's not the number of times you failed that matters most, it's how many times you picked yourself back up.
~ Brené Brown

Could you imagine leading an organization where this mindset was the prevailing way to think about failure?

After many years and many sessions, I began to anticipate what would be asked of me. This book is an attempt to consolidate my ideas, learnings, and thoughts meaningfully; to help others to think differently about their approaches. The goal is to do things in ways that generate better results.

EXAMPLE OF FEAR AND COURAGE AS THE ENABLER?

Jeff L. Engel is a professional nature and wildlife photographer and Amazon bestseller. Here is his example of courage and facing failure.

Being comfortable is as much a part of courage as being brave. Anybody can do something if the outcome will be great. If you are uncertain of the outcome and you do it anyway, however, that is courage. When given the choice of flight or fight, it is courage that says go ahead, give it a try.

Commonly Asked Questions

Courage is visualizing where you want to be in the future, and courage can be stepping out of your comfort zone, even when you really do not want to. With courage, failure may be a possibility, and it takes courage to get going and start again. If you are truly passionate about something, it gives you the leap of faith you need to face your fear and be courageous.

I have an acquaintance who is a talent agent in Nashville, Tennessee. He told me a story about a singer who auditioned for him. This happened to be her tenth audition with a talent agency. After her audition, he told her, "You have no talent." She then went to an eleventh talent agency, and they gave her a chance. She blossomed into a world-class recording artist. She is the epitome of believing in yourself. One of my favorite expressions is, "Fall down 10 times, get up 11." **That is courage.**

Looking back on my life, there have been so many occasions when I have been courageous and did not even realize it. One occasion stands out in particular; selling my successful business and pursuing my creative interests in becoming a nature/wildlife photographer and then hosting, organizing and arranging South African safaris. This was one of my biggest personally frightening and courageous acts, completely changing careers at this stage of my life. But at least I was doing something I was passionate about; something that would make me feel like I had a purpose, and honestly, to have a happy and fulfilling life.

If it weren't for my passion for nature, wildlife, and photography, I never would have had the courage to face my fears of uncertain income and uncertain lifestyle to pursue my lifelong desire. Was it scary? Yes! Was it worth it? Yes! This life transition has helped me develop into the person I am now. Courage can fulfill your most wonderful dreams—you just have to make the first step.

Your fear can hold you back, but if you're brave enough to face your fear and courageous enough to take that step, what you can accomplish has no boundaries. Courage can fulfill your most wonderful dreams.

CAN YOU REST ON YOUR LAURELS?

Sorry, you can't rest on your laurels, because if you want to stay relevant, you must be committed to continuous improvement every day. Every day that you do not advance even in the slightest way, someone will pass you. There is, unfortunately, no moment of absolute clarity when you can suddenly relax and hit auto-pilot. Instead, you need to commit yourself to a lifetime of continuous improvement—you are *always* getting a little bit better today than you were yesterday. There is no endpoint, as my good friend Paul Saunders, who is a leadership consultant in London, keeps on reminding me; "better" never stops.

So celebrate your leadership victories as you achieve them, but never let your guard down or rest on your laurels, because the world is always accelerating ahead.

CONCLUSION

1. SIMPLE FORMULA FOR CHANGE

The formula for positive change consists of this simple equation along with the courage to execute.

Reality + Response = Results

Reality

The courageous leader can change this element—not only for themselves but also for the people they lead. Interpretations can be modified to have more relevance as perception is perceived as reality. While all interpretations are valuable, not all interpretations are equally powerful.

Response

If you have the **ability** to inspire people, to solve problems, the right combination of IQ on the intellectual side and EQ on the "softer" side of leadership, then the big question comes down to what is your **response**?

> **COURAGE IS NOT SIMPLY ONE OF THE VIRTUES, BUT THE FORM OF EVERY VIRTUE AT THE TESTING POINT.**
>
> — C.S. LEWIS

> "SIMPLICITY BOILS DOWN TO TWO STEPS: IDENTIFY THE ESSENTIAL. ELIMINATE THE REST."
> - LEO BABAUTA

Courage comes into place as it connects to the most important 14-letter word in the leadership lexicon. **Responsibility**.

I first perceived the courage-related components of this word while watching the film *Music Within*, the life story of Richard Pimentel. Richard is a disability rights activist who created significant training materials designed to help employers integrate persons with disabilities into the workplace. Richard was a strong advocate for passage of the Americans with Disabilities Act, and that took courage.

The big learning I had was when he broke the Responsibility word into the two words of Response and Ability and then asked the following question; "When you have the ability, what is your response?"

This relationship between our ability to do the right thing and our response to how we are going to permanently solve social injustice is going to take incredible courage by so many people. As Fr. Dan Riley stated in his testimonial in the beginning of this book, the quote from St. Francis of Assisi is a very relevant and courageous call to action to the leaders in our country. "Up until now we have done very little, *let us begin again*." I would add that we all be courageous and do it right this time. This is also a time for our voices to be heard since silence can be perceived as a betrayal.

> "IN THE END, WE WILL REMEMBER NOT THE WORDS OF OUR ENEMIES, BUT THE SILENCE OF OUR FRIENDS."
> - MARTIN LUTHER KING

This is only the end of the beginning…

… so let me end the way we began. My colleague John Wisdom asked you to imagine courage becoming an abundant,

Conclusion

empowering, transformative constant in your life. Now that you've seen what courage is and how and why it matters (i.e., framework), where would you like the impact of your courage to begin? What "tiny habits" (B.J. Fogg) are you prepared to start putting in place *today* to "move the needle" and make a positive difference in your world? How can you courageously inspire others to join you in impacting the world even *more*—regardless of scale, position, or background?

The goal of this second book under the Four Loop Learning foundation was to provide you with new ways to help you think about and become a more courageous leader. We hope that you gained some new insights delineated by the COURAGE acronym.

Change management as a core competency

Overcome mental chatter

Use influence

Relentlessly connect to people's hearts

Always look to improve

Get really good at implementation

Encourage iteration, not perfection

To quote Ernest Hemingway, "COURAGE is grace under pressure." We hope that this seven-letter interpretation of courage provides you with some new perspectives on the importance of courage and increases your grace under pressure.

I wanted to end this book with a prayer that was given to me by my friend Bob Halperin. The prayer provided me with a great perspective on courage in my journey with cancer; we need this perspective now to heal the wrongdoings and injustices in our world.

I asked for strength … and God gave me difficulties to make me strong.

I asked for wisdom … and God gave me problems to solve.

I asked for prosperity … and God gave me brawn and brain to work.

*I asked for **courage** … and God gave me dangers to overcome.*

I asked for patience … and God placed me in situations where I was forced to wait.

I asked for love … and God gave me troubled people to help.

I asked for favors … and God gave me opportunities.

I received nothing I wanted,

I received everything I needed.

MY PRAYER HAS BEEN ANSWERED.

~excerpts from an anonymous soldier's prayer

Wishing you the best of courage!

Bob Cancalosi & Alessandra Cancalosi
https://www.fourlooplearning.com/

NOTES

[1] Perry, Mark J., "Fortune 500 firms in 1955 vs. 2014; 88% are gone, and we're all better off because of that dynamic 'creative destruction'," blog post, AEIdeas, American Enterprise Institute, August 18, 2014 (accessed online on July 25, 2020; http://www.aei.org/publication/fortune-500-firms-in-1955-vs-2014-89-are-gone-and-were-all-better-off-because-of-that-dynamic-creative-destruction/)

[2] Foster, Richard N., and Kaplan, Sarah, *Creative Destruction: Why Companies That Are Built to Last Underperform the Market— And How to Successfully Transform Them*, 2001, Currency; Reprint edition (April 3, 2001); Also see: Foster, Richard N., *Innovation: The Attacker's Advantage*, Summit Books (January 1, 1988).

[3] Schilling, David Russell, "Knowledge Doubling Every 12 Months, Soon to be Every 12 Hours," Industry Tap, April 19, 2013 (accessed online on July 25, 2020; http://www.industrytap.com/knowledge-doubling-every-12-months-soon-to-be-every-12-hours/3950)

[4] Clement, J., "Worldwide digital population as of July 2020," Statistica, July 24, 2020 (accessed online July 25, 2020; https://www.statista.com/statistics/617136/digital-population-worldwide/).

[5] The Ministry of Defense UK, *Strategic Trends Programme Global Strategic Trends - Out to 2045*, Global Strategic Trends, fifth edition, p. 57; benchmarked April 30, 2014; accessed online July 25, 2020; http://www.ieee.es/Galerias/fichero/OtrasPublicaciones/Internacional/2014/Global_Strategic_Trends_-_Out_to_2045.pdf; also available at www.gov.uk/development-concepts-and-doctrine-centre

[6] "Big demands and high expectations: The Deloitte Millennial Survey," Deloitte, January 2014, p. 2; accessed online July 25, 2020; https://www2.deloitte.com/content/dam/Deloitte/global/Documents/About-Deloitte/gx-dttl-2014-millennial-survey-report.pdf

[7] Carol A., "Unilever CEO Sees Purpose-Led Businesses Only Gaining Relevance," *Bloomberg Businessweek*; accessed online July 25, 2020; https://www.bloomberg.com/news/features/2020-05-12/unilever-ceo-on-coronavirus-pandemic-purpose-led-businesses

[8] Brene Brown, May 28, 2020 Commencement Speech Transcript at UT at 1:40 into her 20 minute speech, https://www.rev.com/blog/transcripts/brene-brown-commencement-speech-transcript-for-ut

[9] "How You Can Use the Elephant and the Rider to Motivate Your Team," Lighthouse (blog); accessed online August 1, 2020; https://getlighthouse.com/blog/the-elephant-and-the-rider-motivate-your-team/

[10] Mankins, Michael, and Steele, Richard, "Turning Great Strategy into Great Performance," *Harvard Business Review*; accessed online August 1, 2020; https://hbr.org/2005/07/turning-great-strategy-into-great-performance

[11] Kotter, John, "Leading Change: Why Transformation Efforts Fail," *Harvard Business Review*, May-June 1995; accessed online August 1, 2020: https://hbr.org/1995/05/leading-change-why-transformation-efforts-fail-2

Notes

[12] Sonnad, Nikhil, "You probably won't remember this, but the 'forgetting curve' theory explains why learning is hard," Quartz, February 18, 2018; accessed online August 1, 2020: https://qz.com/1213768/the-forgetting-curve-explains-why-humans-struggle-to-memorize/

[13] Grenny, Joseph, and Patterson, Kerry, *Influencer: The New Science of Leading Change*, McGraw-Hill Education, 2013, p. 166.

[14] Ibid.

Tinka tinka sukh (Happiness lies in small things) was a 104 episode entertainment-education radio soap opera broadcast in India from Februarys 1996.
https://www.routledge.com/Entertainment-Education-A-Communication-Strategy-for-Social-Change-1st/Singhal-Rogers/p/book/9780805833508

Rogers, Everett M, *Diffusion of Innovations, Fourth Edition*, Free Press, 1995;

https://www.amazon.com/Diffusion-Innovations-Fourth-Everett-Rogers/dp/0029266718/

[15] Gladwell, Malcolm, *Outliers: The Story of Success*, Little, Brown and Company, 2008, p. 38; also see: Gladwell, Malcolm, "Complexity and the Ten-Thousand-Hour Rule," *The New Yorker*, August 21, 2013; accessed online August 1, 2020; https://www.newyorker.com/sports/sporting-scene/complexity-and-the-ten-thousand-hour-rule

[16] Kosteniuk, Alexandra, "Kosteniuk Chess Photo surfaces after 23 years," Alexandra Kosteniuk's CHESSQUEEN.COM (blog), October 14, 2014; accessed online August 1, 2020; http://chessqueen.com/kosteniuk-chess-photo-surfaces-after-13-years.html

[17] Sullivan, James, "The Key To Life – Running & Reading?" The Drive Group (blog), May 21, 2020; accessed online August 1, 2020; https://www.thedrivegroup.com.au/blog/2020/05/the-key-to-life-running-and-reading

[18] **Fanning, Ben**. Comments Off on CAREERS: What **Michelangelo can teach you** about **your** dream **job**. Contributing editor. August 21, 2017; https://www.benfanning.com/writing-a-job-description-the-michelangelo-way/

[19] Parker, Nils, "The Angel in the Marble: Modern Life Lessons from History's Greatest Sculptor," Medium (blog), July 9, 2013; accessed online August 1, 2020; https://medium.com/@nilsaparker/the-angel-in-the-marble-f7aa43f333dc

[20] The Dalai Lama, Howard C. Cutler (2005), *The Art Of Happiness At Work*, p. 25, Hachette UK; accessed online August 1, 2020; https://www.azquotes.com/quote/1358591

[21] Beck, Randall, and Harter, Jim, "Managers Account for 70% of Variance in Employee Engagement," *Gallup Business Journal*, April 21, 2015; accessed online August 1, 2020; https://news.gallup.com/businessjournal/182792/managers-account-variance-employee-engagement.aspx

[22] Buchanan, Lee, "The Things They Do for Love," *Harvard Business Review*, December 2004; accessed online August 1, 2020; https://hbr.org/2004/12/the-things-they-do-for-love

[23] "Why People Leave Managers, not Companies (and what to do about it)," Lighthouse (blog); accessed online August 1, 2020; https://getlighthouse.com/blog/people-leave-managers-not-companies/; also see: Nolan, Tom, "The No. 1 Employee Benefit That No One's Talking About," Gallup Workplace; accessed online August 1, 2020; https://www.gallup.com/workplace/232955/no-employee-benefit-no-one-talking.aspx; for a contrary view, also see: Goler, Lori; Gale, Janelle; Harrington, Brynn; and Grant,

Adam; "Why People Really Quit Their Jobs," *Harvard Business Review*, January 11, 2018; accessed online August 1, 2020; https://hbr.org/2018/01/why-people-really-quit-their-jobs

[24] Gartenberg, Claudine, Andrea Prat, and George Serafeim. "Corporate Purpose and Financial Performance." Harvard Business School Working Paper, No. 17-023, September 2016. Accessed online August 1, 2020; http://nrs.harvard.edu/urn-3:HUL.InstRepos:30903237

[25] Nair, Leena, "In the robot age, are you sure you're a human?" World Economic Forum COVID Action Platform; accessed online August 1, 2020; https://www.weforum.org/agenda/2018/01/in-the-robot-age-are-you-sure-youre-a-human

[26] Baldoni, John, "How to Instill Purpose," *Harvard Business Review*, November 11, 2011; accessed online August 1, 2020; https://hbr.org/2011/11/why-purpose-matters; also see: "How to Lead with Purpose (HBR Special Issue)," *Harvard Business Review*, February 11, 2020; accessed online August 1, 2020; https://store.hbr.org/product/how-to-lead-with-purpose-hbr-special-issue/SPSP20

[27] Levinson, Jay, and Jeannie Levinson, *The Best of Guerrilla Marketing: Guerrilla Marketing Remix*, July 8, 2011, Entrepreneur Press, p. 253.

[28] Carlson, Nicholas, "The Untold Story Of Larry Page's Incredible Comeback," *Business Insider*, April 24, 2014; accessed online August 1, 2020; https://www.businessinsider.com/larry-page-the-untold-story-2014-4

[29] "Business Roundtable Redefines the Purpose of a Corporation to Promote 'An Economy That Serves All Americans'," August 19, 2019; accessed online August 1, 2020; https://www.businessroundtable.org/business-roundtable-redefines-the-purpose-of-a-corporation-to-promote-an-economy-that-serves-all-americans

[30] Bjerke, Joshua, "Aon Hewitt Announces List of Top Companies for Leaders," November 26, 2014; accessed online August 1, 2020; https://www.recruiter.com/i/aon-hewitt-announces-list-of-top-companies-for-leaders/

[31] Deutschendorf, Harvey, "Why Emotionally Intelligent People Are More Successful," Fast Company, June 22, 2015; accessed online August 1, 2020; https://www.fastcompany.com/3047455/why-emotionally-intelligent-people-are-more-successful

[32] Axelrod, Joshua, "Corporate Honesty and Climate Change: Time to Own Up and Act," NRDC, February 26, 2019; accessed online August 29, 2020; https://www.nrdc.org/experts/josh-axelrod/corporate-honesty-and-climate-change-time-own-and-act

[33] Domonoske, Camila, "Better Late Than Never? Big Companies Scramble To Make Lofty Climate Promises," NPR, February 27, 2020; accessed online August 29, 2020; https://www.npr.org/2020/02/27/806011419/better-late-than-never-big-companies-scramble-to-make-lofty-climate-promises

[34] "Climate Business | Business Climate," *Harvard Business Review*, October 2007; accessed online August 29, 2020; https://hbr.org/2007/10/climate-business-_-business-climate

[35] Murray, Tom, "The Businesses That Are – And Are Not – Leading On Climate Change," *Forbes*, November 8, 2019; accessed online August 29, 2020; https://www.forbes.com/sites/edfenergyexchange/2019/11/08/the-businesses-that-are--and-are-not--leading-on-climate-change/#7ee698057aa1

[36] *CEO Magazine*, Executive MBA Council **Survey** Results Show Graduates are More Desirable as Rapid Changes to Industries and Globalization Increase. Oct 11, 2017.

Notes

[37] Zenger, John H., and Joseph R. Folkman. "Chapter 14 – The Importance of Follow-through." *The Extraordinary Leader: Turning Good Managers into Great Leaders*, Revised and Expanded Edition. McGraw-Hill, 2009.

[38] "Repeat to Remember, Remember to Repeat," Brain Rules (blog), July 11, 2008; accessed online August 1, 2020; https://brainrules.blogspot.com/2008/07/repeat-to-remember-remember-to-repeat.html

[39] "The Power of Habit Chapter 4 Summary," zipzep (blog); accessed online August 1, 2020; https://zipzep.wordpress.com/2013/09/20/the-power-of-habit-chapter-4-summary/; also see: Duhigg, Charles, *The Power of Habit: Why We Do What We Do in Life and Business*, Chapter 4 (pp. 97-126), Random House, 2012.

[40] "Cost of Delay," ProductPlan; accessed online August 1, 2020; https://www.productplan.com/glossary/cost-of-delay/ also see: Reinertsen, Donald G., *The Principles of Product Development Flow: Second Generation Lean Product Development*, Celeritas Publishing, 2009.

[41] Henry, Todd, *The Accidental Creative: How to Be Brilliant at a Moment's Notice*, p. 203, Portfolio, 2013.

[42] Henry, Todd, *Die Empty: Unleash Your Best Work Every Day*, p. 89, Portfolio. 2013. Also see: Pillemer, Karl, Ph.D., *30 Lessons for Living: Tried and True Advice from the Wisest Americans*, Hudson Street Press, 2011.

[43] Meister, Jeanne, *Corporate Universities: Lessons in Building a World-Class Work Force*, revised edition, McGraw-Hill Education, 1998. Also see: Stemmle, Connie, "The Learning Retention Pyramid: A Simple Guide," Develop Good Habits (blog), April 2, 2020; accessed online August 1, 2020; https://www.developgoodhabits.com/learning-pyramid/

[44] "What is Spaced Repetition and How Does it Improve Your Memory?" Iris Reading, LLC (blog), June 27, 2019; accessed online August 1, 2020; https://irisreading.com/spaced-repetition-and-improved-memory/; also see: Mace, C.A., *The Psychology of Study*, Penguin, 1969.

[45] Edmondson, Amy C., Richard M. Bohmer and Gary Pisano, "Disrupted Routines: Effects of Team Learning on New Technology Adaptation," *Harvard Business School*, July 2000; accessed online August 1, 2020; https://www.hbs.edu/faculty/Publication%20Files/01-003_56f33d92-b538-48e0-938f-f2cc99d90dda.pdf; also see: Edmondson, Amy C., "Strategies for Learning from Failure," *Harvard Business Review*, April 2011; accessed online August 1, 2020; https://hbr.org/2011/04/strategies-for-learning-from-failure

[46] Abrams, JJ (Producer) & Johnson, Rian (Director), 2017 (Motion Picture), *Star Wars: Episode VIII- The Last Jedi Star Wars: The Last Jedi*, United States: Walt Disney Studios Home Entertainment.

[47] Meister, Jeanne, "Three Reasons You Need to Adopt a Millennial Mindset Regardless of Your Age," *Forbes*, October 5, 2012; accessed online August 1, 2020; https://www.forbes.com/sites/jeannemeister/2012/10/05/millennialmindse/#3a1ec02f4ee4

[48] Bump, Philip, "Here Is When Each Generation Begins and Ends, According to Facts," *The Atlantic*, March 25, 2014; accessed online August 1, 2020; http://www.theatlantic.com/national/archive/2014/03/here-is-when-each-generation-begins-and-ends-according-to-facts/359589/; also see: Pew Research Center, "Millennials overtake Baby Boomers as America's largest generation," April 28, 2020; accessed online August 1, 2020; https://www.pewresearch.org/fact-tank/2020/04/28/millennials-overtake-baby-boomers-as-americas-largest-generation/

[49] Pew Research Center, "The Changing Profile of Student Borrowers," October 7, 2014; accessed online August 1, 2020; http://www.pewsocialtrends.org/2014/10/07/the-changing-profile-of-student-borrowers/

Notes

[50] Denning, Tim, "The Future of Leadership—From a Millennial's Perspective," Medium.com (The Startup blog), January 14, 2019; accessed online August 1, 2020; https://medium.com/swlh/the-future-of-leadership-from-a-millennials-perspective-eee766e174e6

[51] "The Ant, the Spider, and the Bee" in Francis Bacon's *The New Organon*, accessed online August 1, 2020; http://www.antspiderbee.net/bacon/

[52] Oppong, Thomas, "The Life-Changing Habit of Journaling (Why Einstein, Leonardo da Vinci, and Many More Great Minds Recommend it)," Medium (Thrive Global blog), June 22, 2017; accessed August 1, 2020; https://medium.com/thrive-global/start-journaling-54ea2edb104

[53] Hutchinson, Bryan, "8 Inspiring Quotes About Writing Everyday (Journal Your Heart Out)," Positive Writer (blog), accessed online August 1, 2020: http://positivewriter.com/8-inspiring-quotes-about-writing-everyday-journal-your-heart-out/

[54] Virginia W. Berninger and Todd L. Richards. *The writing brain: Coordinating sensory/motor, language, and cognitive systems in working memory architecture*. In V. Berninger (Ed.), Past, present, and future contributions of cognitive writing research to cognitive psychology (pp. 537–563). New York, NY: Psychology Press, 2012. Also see: "Handwriting vs. Typing: How to Choose the Best Method to Take Notes," Effectiviology (blog), accessed online August 1, 2020; https://effectiviology.com/handwriting-vs-typing-how-to-take-notes/

[55] "Why is Journaling Important?" Habits for Well-Being (blog), accessed online August 1, 2020; https://www.habitsforwellbeing.com/why-is-journaling-important/

[56] "Repeat to Remember, Remember to Repeat," Brain Rules (blog), July 11, 2008; accessed online August 1, 2020; https://brainrules.blogspot.com/2008/07/repeat-to-remember-remember-to-repeat.html

[57] Willyerd, Karie, *Stretch: How to Future-Proof Yourself for Tomorrow's Workplace*, pp. 46-48, Wiley, 2016.

[58] Zenger, John H., Joseph R. Folkman, Robert H. Sherwin, Jr, & Barbara A. Steel, *How to Be Exceptional: Drive Leadership Success by Magnifying Your Strengths*, McGraw-Hill Education, June 7, 2012.

[59] Cancalosi, Bob, *Four Loop Learning: The Art of Journaling and Reflective Leadership*, P.83. Halo Publishing, 2019.

ACKNOWLEDGEMENTS

John Wisdom is an executive partner who played a pivotal role in helping me create a narrative around Courage. He was more than just a «sounding board»—he pushed me to help "connect the dots" for the many readers wanting to learn more. John has been by my side since the first book, where his communication expertise shaped a solid foundation and dynamic outline, including illuminating examples that made the content come alive. John also wrote the compelling foreword on this book. His lifelong friendship means so much to me.

Andy O'Hearn was a part of my earlier life, when I was just starting to figure out some of the concepts I explore more thoroughly in my books. He has blossomed into an exceptional writer, detailed editor, and expert fact checker. I am so grateful for his contributions to the storyline and his keen editorial skills in making this book come true.

For my **two daughters, Alessandra and Julianne**—Alessandra, this book's co-author, imparted her deep perspective of what courage looks like from the eyes of the generations following mine, and Julianne designed all of the custom graphics for my first and second books, giving Four Loop Learning its distinctive look, feel, and "vibe." Publishing this book infused with the talents of my daughters has been a complete joy. I am immeasurably proud of their valuable contributions.

For my lifelong partner, **Barbara**, who has weathered every storm with me for more than 33 years and has cheered me on to tackle every task others might deem near impossible. No amount of journals could ever capture what we've taken on and learned together. Thank you for every celebration, every sacrifice you embraced so that our family can not only endure, but actually flourish.

And last, but never least, **you**, the reader, and to our **Four Loopers** army. Your thoughts and actions inspire me daily. Thank you so much for sharing your humanity and spreading the word.

If you are interested in learning more about the positive impact of journaling, please go to www.FourLoopLearning.com, where all of the offerings are featured and available for purchase.

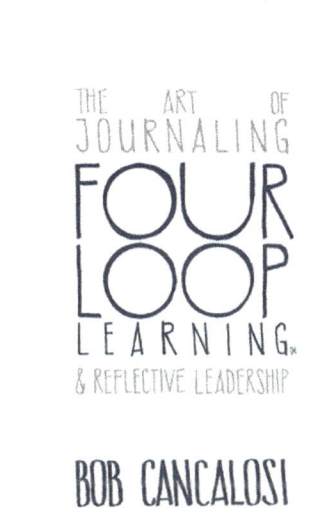

Four Loop Learning:
The Art of Journaling and Reflective Leadership

Paperback
ISBN: 978-1-61244-742-1

Hardcover
ISBN: 978-1-61244-731-5

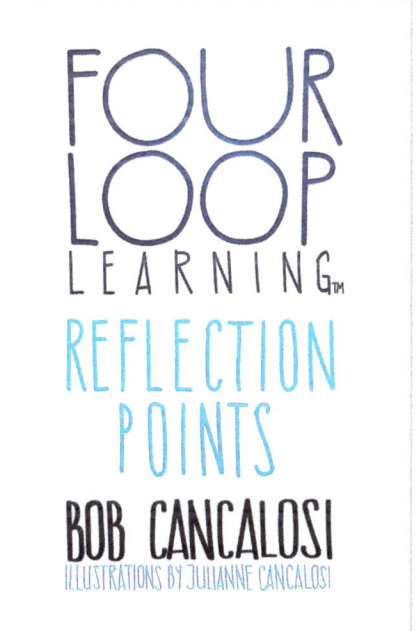

Four Loop Learning:
The Reflections Points Kit

www.ingramcontent.com/pod-product-compliance
Lightning Source LLC
Chambersburg PA
CBHW040436190426
43202CB00041B/2992